Teach Me TORAH

TEACHER'S EDITION

Vicki L. Weber and Sunny Yudkoff

Behrman House, Inc.

Springfield, NJ 07081
www.behrmanhouse.com

Project Editor: Vicki L. Weber
Book Design: Randi Robin Design

ISBN 978-0-87441-827-9

PRINTED THE UNITED STATES OF AMERICA

Table of Contents

Introduction

The *Teach Me Torah Teacher's Edition* gives you tools to teach 16 classic Bible stories along with lessons on Jewish values that are drawn from each. Although not every Bible story in the series is taken literally from the Torah (the first five books of the Bible), *Teach Me Torah* embraces the concept of Torah as sacred teachings in the broad sense.

The *Teacher's Edition* provides a variety of discussion and activity suggestions to help you enhance your students' comprehension of each story and to understand lessons we can all take from it. It will help you use the Teach Me Torah folders as a structured core from which to build lively classroom experiences that begin with the Bible and give your students an appreciation for what Judaism has to teach them about the way they live and the choices they will be making along the way.

This resource is a *guide* to use as you find helpful. Feel free to use the activities and questions provided, to modify the activities as you see fit, and to skip any you feel don't seem right or useful for your own class. You know your students best, and you know how you like to teach.

The Features of *Teach Me Torah*

The purpose of the *Teach Me Torah* series is to bring the dramatic stories of the Bible to life for young students using compelling language accompanied by vibrant illustrations. Once drawn in, students can come to appreciate that, in addition to being intriguing tales, these stories have something to teach us about how to live.

Each folder of *Teach Me Torah* features an illustrated Bible story based closely on the biblical text. The biblical source for the story is provided on the front page of each folder. Elements of each story have been simplified, or in some cases eliminated, in order to present a cogent yet direct story appropriate for early readers. The *Teacher's Edition* also offers the feature "Teach Me MORE Torah" that provides supplemental information about many of the stories presented.

An activity on page three of each folder is designed to reinforce comprehension of the Bible story. The feature "My D'var Torah" then introduces and explains a key value related to the text and provides a thought question for further discussion. A second activity, found on page four of each folder, is designed to further students' understanding of the value.

Each *Teach Me Torah* folder concludes with "Ask at Home," a thought-provoking, open-ended question you can use to begin a class discussion. Send the folders home with your students, and encourage them to continue the discussion by posing the question to parents or siblings. You may wish to begin the next class with a recap of this question, asking your students to share some of the ways in which their families answered last week's question.

The activities provided in the *Teach Me Torah* folders can be completed individually by your students with crayons or pencils, or you can ask students to point out answers with their fingers. In addition, these activities can generally be adapted from individual, paper-based exercises to small group projects or to a broader, class wide discussion, depending upon students' abilities and your preferences as a teacher.

The Features of the *Teach Me Torah Teacher's Edition*

Each *Teach Me Torah* folder is self-contained and the *Teacher's Edition* provides a wealth of additional features, such as background information for the teacher, supplemental questions for promoting comprehension and vibrant class discussion, as well as ideas for hands-on activities that help you use each folder as the core element of a multi-dimensional classroom experience.

The *Teacher's Edition* provides a mixture of straightforward recall questions to help young students review the story for content, and more open-ended questions intended to promote understanding in a broader context. Hints and answers for all the activities in *Teach Me Torah* are also provided throughout the *Teacher's Edition.*

In this *Teacher's Edition* you will find reproductions of the actual pages of each folder. A lesson plan for each folder is provided, containing the following elements:

- **Overview:** Places the story in context and provides background.
- **Core Concept:** Provides essential information about the story's key themes.
- **Objectives:** Outlines learning goals of the lesson.
- **Words to Know:** Highlights terms that may be difficult for young readers.
- **Getting Started:** Designed to be used just before distribution of the folder, or just before reading the story, these activities will help you introduce the story and its themes to your students.
- **Using the Illustration (1 and 2):** Helps you make the most of the artwork featured throughout the folders by providing ideas and questions that can help your students engage with the material in a visual way, aiding their comprehension.
- **Teaching the Story:** Provides you with questions to further your students' understanding of the text, and guides you through the comprehension activity on page three of each folder, including offering ideas for using it in small groups or as a whole class.
- **Teach Me MORE Torah:** Provides additional information—either background about the Bible story, explanations of the text, or elements of the story that were not included in the folder—that you can use to enrich your students' experience.
- **Bring the Story to Life:** Provides ideas for a hands-on activity or craft project based on the elements of the story.
- **My D'var Torah:** Expands on the values lesson introduced in the folder, provides some additional thought questions, and guides you through the activity provided on page four of each folder.
- **Bring the Value to Life:** Provides ideas for a classroom project or group activity that focuses on the value presented in the folder.
- **Ask at Home:** Provides suggestions for using the photograph as a discussion starter as well as additional questions to make the most out of this feature.

Scope and Sequence

Each *Teach Me Torah* folder tells a classic Bible story and highlights a Jewish value that students can draw from the story and connect to their own lives.

Set One

Folder	Story	Value	Core Concept
1	**God and Creation**	Taking Care of the World	We are partners with God in creation and must help take care of nature.
2	**Adam and Eve**	Accepting Responsibility	Growing up means learning from our mistakes and thinking about our actions.
3	**Noah**	Doing the Right Thing	We must try to make the right decisions, even when those around us do not. Rules can help guide our behavior by reminding us of the right choices.
4	**Tower of Babel**	Remembering to be Humble	When we remember to be humble, we become mindful of what is within our control and what is beyond our human reach.
5	**Abraham**	Standing Up for Others	We should speak up for others so that they are treated fairly and as we would wish to be treated.
6	**Rebecca**	Showing Kindness	It is important to act kindly toward all of God's creatures, people and animals alike.
7	**Jacob and Esau**	Keeping Peace in Your Family	We should respect and value our family members in order to bring about *sh'lom bayit*—peace in our homes and with our families.
8	**Joseph**	Asking for Forgiveness	Asking for forgiveness and admitting our mistakes is hard, but apologizing helps us bring peace into our lives.

Set Two

Folder	Story	Value	Core Concept
9	**Miriam and Moses**	Protecting Life	Each of us can help make another person's life happy, healthy, and safe.
10	**Moses and Pharaoh**	Trusting in God	Our belief and trust in God carries us through difficult times and helps us overcome personal challenges.
11	**The Israelites and God's Laws**	Serving God	By following God's commandments, we learn how to treat others with respect and love.
12	**Ruth and Naomi**	Feeding the Hungry	We must make sure that all Jewish people have food and shelter and that all newcomers feel welcome in our community.
13	**David and Goliath**	Being Brave	Our trust in God and support from our friends give us courage.
14	**Solomon**	Seeking Wisdom	When we seek out wisdom, we learn to act justly and make fair decisions.
15	**Jonah**	Caring About Others	We must care about others, even those who do not act as we wish. We also must forgive others when they repent.
16	**Esther**	Loyalty to the Jewish People	*Kol Yisrael areivim zeh bazeh*—All Jewish people are responsible for one another.

Incorporating *Teach me Torah* into Your Curriculum

The sixteen Bible stories of *Teach Me Torah* can be covered over the course of one school year with plenty of time left for special holiday programs and other curricular topics and goals. The folders provide the materials to introduce weekly Bible study into your supplementary school class in ways you can easily modify according to the time you have available, by adding additional questions and activities from this *Teacher's Edition.*

The following techniques outline three general ways to incorporate the *Teach Me Torah* folders into your classroom curriculum:

1. ***Teach Me Torah:* Shabbat Tales**
   a. For those teachers using *Teach Me Torah* in a weekday program, you can use the folders to make studying Torah part of your class's Shabbat celebration. Reserve time every week before Shabbat to review the story and complete the activities of a *Teach Me Torah* folder. By using the folders close to Shabbat and late in the week, you will be able to send folders home with the students over the weekend while the material is fresh in their memories.

2. ***Teach Me Torah:* This Week's Parashah**
   a. You can coordinate a Teach Me Torah folder with the weekly Torah portion *(parashah)* from which it is taken. Below is a table that shows which *parashah* corresponds to each folder. Some folders include material from more than one *parashah.* Alternatively, some Torah portions include material that fills more than one folder. The following stories have a corresponding *parashah:*

Folder	Story	Parashah
1	God and Creation	*Bereisheet*
2	Adam and Eve	*Bereisheet*
3	Noah	*Noaḥ*
4	Tower of Babel	*Noaḥ*
5	Abraham	*Lech Lecha*
6	Rebecca	*Ḥayei Sarah*
7	Jacob and Esau	*Toldot, VaYishlaḥ*
8	Joseph	*VaYeshev, Mikeitz, VaYigash*
9	Miriam and Moses	*Shmot*
10	Moses and Pharaoh	*Shmot, VaYera, Bo, BeShallaḥ*
11	The Israelites and God's Laws	*Yitro, Mishpatim*
14	Solomon	*Mikeitz (haftarah)*

3. *Teach Me Torah:* Holiday Preparation

a. You can enrich a lesson about a Jewish holiday with a *Teach Me Torah* folder. The folders below explore biblical texts that we read on specific holidays. Note that not all the folders are listed.

Folder	Story	Holiday
1	**God and Creation**	*Simḥat Torah*
2	**Adam and Eve**	*Simḥat Torah*
10	**Moses and Pharaoh**	*Passover*
11	**The Israelites and God's Laws**	*Shavuot*
12	**Ruth and Naomi**	*Shavuot*
15	**Jonah**	*Yom Kippur*
16	**Esther**	*Purim*

A Special Note on Answering Tough Questions—Is It True?

Young children can be quite literal thinkers. Many accept Bible stories as truth. Others will ask: Did God *really* create the world in six days? Did a huge fish *really* swallow Jonah? What can we tell them? Of course, some people do treat the Torah as literal truth. Others believe that the Torah uses metaphorical language to teach important lessons. And while some people believe science and Torah are in conflict, we must remember that in the history of classical biblical commentary, questions of the truth of specific details such as how many years one person lived or exactly how long creation took were inconsequential. We must acknowledge that it is difficult for us to harmonize modernity with the ancient mind. We can remember, however, that while science today looks for explanations of how the world came to be, biblical stories bear deep spiritual insights about the role of people in the world, and the values we should try to live by—ideas you will be exploring with your students this year.

The language of *Teach Me Torah* allows students the freedom to form their own opinions. In the Bible stories themselves, and in the **"My D'var Torah"** features, the direct actions of God and biblical personalities are described as they appear in the Torah. This is distinct from the syntax of the **"Ask at Home"** questions, which invite inquiry about what "the Torah tells us," or what "our tradition says," thus allowing the interpretation that the Torah relates universal truths without being necessarily literal. You may wish to acknowledge that it is perfectly acceptable not to be sure what you believe, and that each of us develops our own ideas over time.

Working with Varied Learning Styles and Special Needs

Learning styles vary greatly among children. Some learn best with a visual or auditory approach; others learn best when provided with opportunities for hands-on activities. Teachers who present material in a variety of ways will be able to reach more children more effectively.

Teachers of children with special needs face additional challenges. Their students have a wide range of physical, behavioral, and cognitive disabilities that can greatly affect both their own learning and the classroom. Talking to parents about the accommodations made in a student's secular classroom can be helpful. The suggestions below are primarily designed for students with learning, perceptual, or attention problems.

- For children with attention and auditory processing difficulties, material is most effectively presented in small increments. Give one instruction at a time and ask the student to repeat the instruction to ensure comprehension.
- For children with attention deficits, limit teaching segments to 10 to 15 minutes, and allow for movement between activities. Some children with attention challenges do well when allowed to stand or to hold a prop during discussions.
- For children with attention and visual figure-ground problems, mask parts of the page so they can see only the section being discussed. The sections of *Teach Me Torah* are presented in blocks, making them easy to mask.

The amount of writing and drawing is limited in *Teach Me Torah,* making it appropriate for students with attention deficits or with limited fine motor or handwriting skills. The *Teacher's Edition* also provides alternatives for completing the activities of the folders in small, collaborative groups, or as a class, to minimize or even eliminate any need for the students to write themselves. In crafting additional in-class activities, plan for a teacher or assistant to do difficult or time-consuming parts of a project and then allow the student to finish the task.

Help students complete assignments in ways that are compatible with their learning styles and skill levels. For example, students may wish to complete a word search by outlining a word with a finger rather than a pencil or by pointing to objects in a drawing rather than circling items. You can have the whole class help find a hidden word by writing the letters on the board as the students find them and call them out.

Parent Letters

You can copy the following parent letters onto your school's letterhead and send them out just as you begin each new set of *Teach Me Torah* Bible folders. The letter on page 13 covers Set One. The letter on page 15 covers Set Two.

Dear Parent,

We are beginning some Bible study in our class. Over the coming weeks we will be reading eight Bible stories together, learning both about significant biblical figures from our tradition and about a key Jewish value illuminated by each story. The stories are all taken from texts in Genesis, beginning with the story of creation and taking us up through the time of the Israelites following Joseph to Egypt.

The stories we will use are from Behrman House's *Teach Me Torah 1* series of Bible folders. Each folder contains one story, along with thought questions and activities that we will cover in class. At the end of each class, your child will bring the folder home so you can read it together.

Over the course of our study we will be reading:

God and Creation	*Abraham*
Adam and Eve	*Rebecca*
Noah	*Jacob and Esau*
Tower of Babel	*Joseph*

The biblical reference for each story is given, and each story stays as close as possible to the text while still remaining age-appropriate.

On the back page of each folder you will find an "Ask at Home" feature, an open-ended question, based on the lessons of the story, that your child may enjoy discussing with you. We have begun the discussion of the "Ask at Home" question in class. These are thought questions, by and large, and no special knowledge of the Bible is needed to have an engaging talk with your child.

Dear Parent,

Over the coming weeks we will be reading eight Bible stories together, learning both about significant biblical figures from our tradition and about a key Jewish value illuminated by each story. The stories include several from the book of Exodus as well as later books of the Bible

We will be using story folders from Behrman House's *Teach Me Torah 2* series. Each folder contains one story, along with thought questions and activities that we will cover in class. At the end of each class, your child will bring the folder home so you can read it together.

Over the course of our study we will be reading:

Miriam and Moses	*David and Goliath*
Moses and Pharaoh	*Solomon*
The Israelites and God's Laws	*Jonah*
Ruth and Naomi	*Esther*

The biblical reference for each story is given, and each story stays as close as possible to the text while still remaining age-appropriate.

On the back page of each folder you will find an "Ask at Home" feature, an open-ended question, based on the lessons of the story, that your child may enjoy discussing with you. We have begun the discussion of the "Ask at Home" question in class. These are thought questions, by and large, and no special knowledge of the Bible is needed to have an engaging talk with your child.

Teach Me TORAH 1

God and Creation

Genesis 1:1–2:3

When God began to create the heavens and the earth, everything was wild and dark.

God said, "Let there be light." God called the light Day, and the darkness, Night. The evening came, and then the morning. It was the first day.

"Let there be sky," God said, and the heavens separated from the world below. The evening came, and then the morning. It was the second day.

Teach Me TORAH 1

WORDS TO KNOW

Create—make

Creation—the act of making. Also, the world and everything in it.

Getting Started

You will need blank sheets of paper and round self adhesive stickers/labels in a variety of colors (available at most office supply stores). Give each student a sheet of paper and several sheets of stickers. Tell them to make "something" using only the circle stickers. Have the students share their creations. Next, show them how to make a flower out of stickers. When they have made flowers of their own, ask: would you have made it this way without directions? Explain that just as they needed directions, or plans, to make the flower, a builder needs plans to build a house or a bridge. And God had a plan when making the world.

Using the Illustration

After reading the story, turn back to the first page and ask individual students to find the elements of each day of creation. Where is it "wild and dark" in the illustration? Where is the sun shining? Where is it night? What animals can they find? Can they name all the animals?

Fun question: Can they find the turtle in the illustration? What day would they say turtles were created? *(Students can make a case for the fifth day, when the biblical text says "sea creatures and all living creatures of every kind that creep," the sixth day ("crawling things"), or even BOTH days—sea turtles and land turtles.)*

Overview

The beginning of the book of Genesis describes each of the six days of God's creation of the world and the seventh day of rest.

Core Concept

Creation took place according to a plan. As part of that plan, people, whom God said will "rule over the whole earth," have a special mission to take care of God's other creations.

Objectives

Students will be able to:

- Name what was created on each of the six days
- Relate the phrase "rule over the whole earth" to taking care of creation
- Connect the value of taking care of the world with everyday activities that reflect this value.
- Explore the idea that Creation was planned, not haphazard, and that each of God's creations has a role to play in the larger world.

Teaching the Story

Q. **What did God make first?** *(Light; named day and night)*

Q. **What did God do on the second day? What did God do on the second day?** *(Made the sky)*

Q. **God separated dry land from the seas on the third day, and created plants, before creating any animals. What would have happened if the land animals had been created BEFORE the dry land?** *(They could not live without dry land to walk on and plants to eat. The order of creation was important.)*

Q. **What kinds of animals did God create on the fifth day, and what kind on the sixth day?** *(On the fifth day, God created the animals of the seas and the sky—fish and birds. On the sixth day, God created the animals of the earth—beasts and crawling things.)*

Q. **When did God create people?** *(God created people on the sixth day, after all the animals.)*

Q. **Why were people created last?** *(To show them all that the world offered them, and to show them everything they would rule over and care for.)*

Q. **God rested on the seventh day and made the day holy. What is this holy day?** *(Shabbat)*

"Let there be dry land, and seas," said God. "Let plants and trees grow on the land." The evening came, and then the morning. It was the third day.

"Let there be lights in the sky," said God. "The sun will shine in the daytime, the moon and stars at night." The evening came, and then the morning. It was the fourth day.

God said, "Let the seas fill with fish. Let birds fly in the sky." The evening came, and then the morning. It was the fifth day.

"Let there be animals," said God, "tame ones, and wild beasts, and crawling things. Let there be people. They will rule over the whole earth." The evening came, and then the morning. It was the sixth day.

Then God blessed the seventh day and made it holy. It was the day God rested after creating the world.

2

Teach Me MORE Torah

Most ancient peoples told creation stories. Some important differences between those stories and ours include the sense that God had a plan for creation, and that this plan included a central role for people by charging them with overseeing or taking care of creation, rather than simply serving human-like gods (a feature of Babylonian creation stories, for example). And while other early creation stories may have suggested a day of rest, none gave it the divine creation described in the Torah.

Counting the Days

Draw a line from each number to the picture showing what was created that day.

1 2 3 4 5 6

Taking Care of the World

What does it mean to rule over the earth?

A good ruler can be like a parent. A parent takes care of all members of the family. By taking care of the world the way parents take care of a family, people can rule the earth.

How can you help take care of the world?

3

Using the Illustration

What are the hands doing? *(Protecting the world; taking care of the world)*

Why are the hands all different colors? *(It takes all kinds of people to take care of the world. The world is filled with many different peoples.)*

Counting the Days

If you have an extra folder, you can cut out the individual creation illustrations and have students work together or as a class to put the squares in order. If you have access to a color copier, you can create story board squares for the entire class (put two sets of squares on the same sheet to save paper).

Bring the Story to Life: The Days of Creation

Divide the students into six groups. Assign each group a day of creation, beginning with Day Two. Supply students with markers and paper to draw what God created on their day. Tell the students that each group will show their creation in order.

To begin, let yourself be Day One. Turn off the classroom lights and announce, "On the first day, God created ..." Pause, turn on the lights, and continue, "Light. On the second day, God created ..." Turn to the second day group, and ask them to stand up and present their creations. Continue through all the days

My D'var Torah: Talking Care of the World

As the class discusses ways to take care of the world, you can explain *Tikkun Olam*, the Jewish tradition of repairing the world. It is part of our tradition to make the world a better place.

Help Take Care of Creation

If no one chooses the computer, ask students how this family might use a computer to take care of the world.

Bring the Value to Life: Recycling Teams

Divide the class into recycling teams. Give each team an item that can be recycled, such as a small cardboard box or plastic bottle. Challenge each team to brainstorm other uses for their object. Then let teams demonstrate novel uses. Encourage students to think of Jewish uses, such as turning water bottles into Purim graggers.

Help Take Care of Creation

Help this family take care of the world.

Circle three things from below that will help them.

Why did you choose these ones?

Ask at Home

The Torah says God created crawling things.

Why do you think the Torah includes crawling things, like ants and spiders?

4

Story Illustration: Giovannina Colalillo; Activity Illustration: Bot Roda; Photo: image 100/Corbis; Printed in China; ISBN-10: 0-87441-825-9; ISBN-13: 978-0-87441-825-5.

Ask at Home

Begin with the photograph of the spider. You may or may not wish to point out that the spider has caught an insect. In eliciting answers from the students, point out that animals such as spiders and insects have intriguing, and often unappreciated, jobs in the world: as nature's janitors, as food for other animals, even as a way to appreciate beauty (think of butterflies and lightning bugs).

By considering the role of "crawling things" in the Torah, we can learn to appreciate the role every creature plays in the world as part of God's plan.

Teach Me TORAH 2

Adam and Eve

Genesis 2:4–3:24

Adam, the first man, and Eve, the first woman, lived in a garden called Eden.

Fruit trees of all kinds grew in Eden. "You may eat any fruit in the garden except one," God said. "Do not eat fruit from the Tree of Knowledge of Good and Evil. If you do, you will die."

Overview

The story of Adam and Eve and the snake can be understood as an allegory about the battle between good and evil in all of us. We all make choices between right and wrong, and we need to understand that these choices come with consequences.

Core Concept

Growing up means learning from our mistakes and thinking about our actions.

Objectives

Students will be able to:

- Name the first man and woman
- Recount a timeline for the story
- Relate the freedom to choose with the idea that choices have consequences
- Explore God's concern for Adam and Eve even as they were being punished

Teach Me TORAH 2

WORDS TO KNOW

Adam—Hebrew for "person." Adam's name is related to the Hebrew word for clay or earth, *adamah*. The Torah tells us that God formed Adam from clay.

Eve—derives from the Hebrew word for "life"

Hardship—trouble, suffering

Getting Started

Everyone can remember a story from childhood of doing something wrong (and sometimes, of getting caught in the process). Tell the students one of your own stories, and ask for volunteers to do the same. Ask students how they felt about what they did, and what happened as a result. Did they learn anything?

Using the Illustration

After reading the story, have students turn back to the illustration on the front page. Ask them to find elements from the story. Can they find fruit trees? Can they find the snake? What kind of life did Adam and Eve have in Eden? Would they have been hungry if they did not eat the fruit God told them not to eat?

Teaching the Story

Q. What were the names of the people in the garden?
(Adam and Eve)

Q. What did God tell Adam and Eve about the Tree of Knowledge of Good and Evil?
(God told them not to eat fruit from that tree. God told them they would die if they ate its fruit.)

Q. Why did Adam and Eve eat the fruit?
(The fruit looked delicious and the snake told Eve she would not die if she ate it. Eve gave the fruit to Adam.)

Q. Why did Adam and Eve hide when they heard God calling to them?
(They had done what God told them not to do. Now that they had eaten the fruit from the Tree of Knowledge of Good and Evil, they knew they had done something wrong, and they were afraid.)

Q. Who did Adam and Eve blame? *(Adam blamed Eve; Eve blamed the snake.)*

Q. Who did God punish?
(God punished the snake, then God punished Adam and Eve.)

Q. What did God do for Adam and Eve before sending them away from the Garden of Eden?
(God gave them clothing and dressed them so they would be protected.)

A snake also lived in Eden. "You will not die," the snake hissed to Eve. "If you eat the fruit from the Tree of Knowledge you will know good from evil, just like God."

The fruit looked delicious. Eve took a bite. She gave the fruit to Adam. He took a bite, too.

Then Adam and Eve heard God calling to them. They hid behind the trees.

"Why did you hide? God asked. "Did you eat the fruit I told you not to eat?"

"Eve gave it to me," said Adam.

"The snake tricked me," Eve said.

God spoke to the snake. "Because you have done this, you will crawl on your belly and eat dust all the days of your life!"

God spoke to Adam and Eve. "You will face hardship and pain."

Then God dressed Adam and Eve in clothing made from animal skins, and sent them out of the Garden of Eden forever.

2

Teach Me MORE Torah

The Torah does not actually tell us what kind of fruit grew on the Tree of Knowledge of Good and Evil. While it is often depicted as an apple or a pomegranate, many of our sages believed it was a fig. The rabbis identify the fruit as a fig because the Torah tells us that, after Adam and Eve ate of the fruit, they became aware of their own nakedness and they chose fig leaves to cover themselves. You may wish to bring some figs to class for your students to see and taste. Remind students that figs grow in the Land of Israel and throughout the Middle East.

Before and After

When Adam and Eve ate the fruit from the Tree of Knowledge, everything changed. Circle the pictures that show things that happened **after** Adam and Eve disobeyed God.

Accepting Responsibility

Why did God punish Adam and Eve and not just the snake?

The snake did not force Eve to eat the fruit. Eve had a choice. Eve gave Adam fruit. She did not make him eat it. Adam had a choice, too. Adam and Eve tried to hide from God. They tried to blame others for their own mistakes.

What happens when we try to hide from our mistakes?

3

Before and After

You can cut out the illustrations from an extra folder (or copy several sets if you have access to a color copier) and have students work in groups to put the story board in order.

Bring the Story to Life: Corner Garden of Eden

Create your own Garden of Eden. Have students draw people, animals, and plants that would have been in the Garden of Eden. (You can also have students bring in small stuffed animals.) Collect these and hang or place them in a corner of your classroom. Add a stuffed snake and fruit bowl to the corner garden. Use the drawings and props to retell the story of the Garden of Eden.

My D'var Torah: Accepting Responsibility

Remind students how the Torah tells us that Adam and Eve tried to hide among the trees when God called to them. Ask them what happens when we try to hide from our mistakes. *(They don't go away; the problems can grow bigger.)*

Decision Tree

Discuss each of the illustrations in the game of people choosing good and bad behavior. Then let students break up into small groups to play the game. You will need one coin for each group, and small items such as buttons to use as game markers.

Bring the Value to Life: Class Pet

As a class, adopt a (stuffed) animal. Let students name it. Encourage them to choose a Hebrew name. Ask students how they will care for the pet. What will be hard? What will the pet eat? Remind students that God instructed Adam and Eve to name and care for the animals God created, and that humans have a responsibility to treat animals with respect.

Decision Tree

Flip a coin to make your move. Heads moves one space, tails two. As you go, watch for good choices that help you get to the top of the tree. Be careful! The snake landed in the dirt!

Ask at Home

Why do you think the Torah tells us that God dressed Adam and Eve before sending them away from Eden?

4

Ask at Home

Have students begin with the photograph of a father helping to dress his daughter. What is he showing about his feelings for her? *He takes care of her; he loves her.* Explain that in the story God shows love for Adam and Eve even when punishing them. Kindness, even when it is not "earned" or "deserved," is a basic element of Jewish ethical tradition.

Teach Me TORAH 3

Noah

Genesis 6:5–9:17

People had spread evil over all the earth. "I wish I had never created them," God said.

But one man, Noah, was good. Noah walked with God.

"Build an ark, Noah," said God. "Take your family and two of each animal onto the ark. Take food for all." And Noah did what God told him to do.

Overview

The story of Noah describes God's decision to destroy the world because people had become evil. Noah and his family are spared because Noah was the only man in his generation who "walked with God." Noah follows God's command to build an ark and to take his family and animals of every kind onto the ark to save them. After the flood, God blesses Noah, provides seven basic guidelines for human behavior, and promises never again to destroy the earth with a flood.

Core Concept

We should try to make the right decisions even when those around us do not. Rules help guide our behavior by reminding us of the right choices to make.

Objectives

Students will be able to:

- Retell the story of Noah
- Describe what it means to "walk with God"
- Explore the role of rules in guiding behavior

Teach Me TORAH 3

WORDS TO KNOW

Ark—a large wooden boat

Getting Started

Bring one or more prisms to class and pass them around for students to examine. Ask students if they have seen rainbows in the sky. When do rainbows usually appear? *(When the sun shines after it has rained)* Point out that the colors are always in the same order. Ask your students if they knew that there is a special blessing you can say when you see a rainbow. The blessing tells of God's promise to Noah never again to destroy the earth in a flood.

Blessing Upon Seeing a Rainbow

בָּרוּךְ אַתָּה, יְיָ אֱלֹהֵינוּ,
מֶלֶךְ הָעוֹלָם, זוֹכֵר הַבְּרִית,
וְנֶאֱמָן בִּבְרִיתוֹ, וְקַיָּם בְּמַאֲמָרוֹ.

Baruch Atah, Adonai Eloheinu,
Melech ha'olam, zocher habrit,
V'ne'eman bi'vrito, v'kayam b'ma'amaro.

Praised are You, Adonai our God,
Ruler of the world, who remembers the covenant,
And is faithful to God's covenant, and keeps God's word.

Using the Illustration

After reading through the story, have students turn back to the first page. Can they find elements from the story? Do they see the rain? *(Behind the ark)* Where is the sun beginning to shine? *(In front of the ark)* How is the water near the front of the boat different from the water behind the boat? *(Gentler, lighter/brighter, calmer, friendlier)*

A few animals are looking out of the ark. What do the students think it was like INSIDE the ark? Do they see the bird? What does it mean that the bird is carrying leaves in its beak? *(The bird has found a tree, so the waters are beginning to go down)* If they were going to draw a picture of what happened next, what would be in it? *(Dry land; rainbow; Noah and animals coming out of the ark)*

Teaching the Story

Q. **God said "I wish I had never created people." Why?** *(People had spread evil over all the earth.)*

Q. **What made Noah different from the other people of his time?** *(Noah was good. He walked with God.)*

Q. **What is an ark?** *(A very large wooden boat.)*

Q. **Who was on the ark along with Noah?** *(Noah's family and animals of every kind.)*

Q. **How long did it rain?** *(Forty days and nights)*

Q. **What promise did God make to Noah?** *(Never again to destroy the earth with a flood)*

Q. **What is the symbol of God's promise?** *(A rainbow)*

Q. **What else did God give Noah and his family?** *(Rules; God told Noah and his family that they were allowed to kill animals for food but not allowed to kill people.)*

Teach Me MORE Torah 1

The ark was huge: 300 cubits by 50 cubits by 30 cubits (Genesis 6:15). A cubit is about 1½ feet long, so the ark was 450 feet long, 75 feet wide, and 45 feet high. By comparison, a football field is 300 feet long, and three story building is about 45 feet high.

Then it began to rain. For forty days and forty nights the rain poured down. Water rose and covered the earth. Noah's ark floated along, keeping his family and all the animals safe.

The rain stopped. Noah sent birds out of the ark but they flew right back. There was no place to land. There was only water.

After seven days, Noah sent a bird out again. It came back with an olive branch. It had found a tree top that was not covered by water.

The third time Noah sent a bird out, it did not come back. It had found a place to live. The earth was finally dry.

"Come out of the ark," God said to Noah. Then God blessed Noah and his family. God said, "You may kill animals for food. But do not kill people. They are created in the image of God."

"Never again will I destroy the earth with a flood," said God. "I have set a rainbow in the clouds as a sign of My promise."

2

Teach Me MORE Torah 2

The story of Noah actually contains two descriptions of the number of animals God told Noah to bring onto the ark. In the first, Noah is to bring two of each animal, a male and a female (Genesis 6:19). In the second version, Genesis 7:2-3, God commands Noah to bring seven pairs of ritually clean animals, and two each of animals considered to be ritually unclean. Some traditional commentators, such as Rashi, have interpreted the first command to mean "at least two" of each animals. After the flood, when Noah's family leaves the ark, Genesis 8:20 tells us that Noah built an altar and made an offering of some of these ritually clean animals, leading to God's promise never again to destroy the earth.

Using the Illustration 2

Ask students to describe when this is happening—before the flood or after. How can they tell? *(Animals leaving the ark; rainbow; clear skies; Noah being blessed)*. Note that Noah is depicted at an altar, which the Torah tells us he built after emerging from the ark, in order to make a sacrifice. Sacrifices were our ancestors' way of praying to God.

Waiting for a Sign

Noah wanted to know when to leave the ark, so he sent birds out three times. Finish each picture below to show how the world looked each time a bird left the ark.

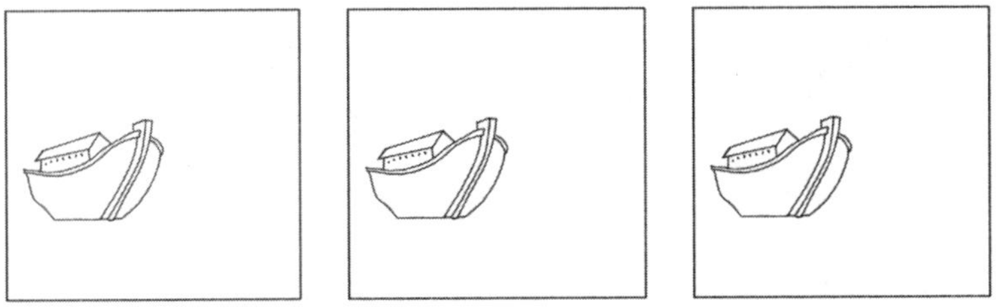

Doing the Right Thing

What does it mean to walk with God?

The Torah tells us that Noah was different from other people. The others did wicked things. Noah set out to do what God asked. By doing the right thing, like taking care of the animals, and by following God's commands, Noah walked with God.

How can you walk with God?

3

Bring the Story Alive: Calling the Animals to the Ark

Draw the outline of an ark on poster board (or make a three-dimensional one using a cardboard box for the bottom and a folded piece of poster board for the roof). Collect pictures of animals from magazines or the Internet. (Search under "animal name + image.") Collect two images of every animal. Try to choose different types of animals: birds, mammals, and insects. Tell students that they, like Noah, must gather together pairs of animals for the ark. Have students close their eyes. Give each student one animal picture. Instruct them that, when you say "two-by-two," they should open their eyes and find the other half of their animal pair. Invite pairs of students to paste their animal pictures on the ark.

You can also have each child "become" his or her animal, and tell a short story about what it was like for that animal to live on the ark with Noah and all the other animals. (This activity can also be done with stuffed animals that each child brings from home.)

Waiting for a Sign

You might discuss this activity together as a class, and have students describe how they would complete each picture. Or, create large-sized versions of the incomplete pictures. Divide the students into three groups and have each group complete its picture together as a team. Each team can then present its work and tell its part of the story. Be sure to point out any rainbows students may have drawn.

Art Project: My Own Rainbow

Use round, basket-type coffee filters, water color markers, a spray bottle with water, and individual 8 ½ x 11 inch sheets of construction paper in a variety of colors. Cut the coffee filters in half to make semi-circles, and flatten. Have each student color a filter with watercolor markers to make a rainbow. Place the completed rainbows on butcher paper or paper plates and mist with the sprayer to make the colors bleed slightly. When dry, glue to construction paper.

My D'var Torah: Doing the Right Thing

Point out to students that one of the ways Noah walked with God was to be sure to take food for all the animals on to the ark. This may give them some practical ideas for applying this lesson to their own lives. *(Doing the right thing even if others are not; taking care of other creatures; taking care of the earth; taking care of each other)*

Walk/Don't Walk

Ask students: What is going wrong here? *(The drivers are not following the rules.)* What will help Ben and Hannah get to school safely? *(The drivers should stop for the red light; drive the right way down the one way street; not park in the crosswalk/ no parking zone.)*

You may also wish to review the rules of your classroom. What rules make the class work smoothly? What would happen if the classroom did not have rules?

Bring the Value to Life: N-O-A-H

Write out the letters N-O-A-H vertically on the black board. Ask students to use the letters of Noah's name to describe what made him a good person. Some answers might include "**N**ice" or "**O**beyed God." Then have each student write his or her name on a piece of paper. Instruct students to use the letters of their own names to write adjectives that describe people who do the right thing.

You may wish to conduct this as a group activity, writing students' names on the board, in turn, and asking for suggestions from the class.

Walk/Don't Walk

What a mess! Ben and Hannah can't get to school because no one is following the rules. Help them out. Circle the clues that help everyone know the rules of the road.

Ask at Home

The Torah tells us God gave rules to Noah's family after the flood. Why are rules important?

4

Ask at Home

Begin by discussing the photo of the boy with the stop sign. Who is he? Why does he have a stop sign? What would happen if people did not follow the rule when he holds up his sign? This can lead to a more general discussion of the value of rules. Why should we follow rules even when no one else is and even when no one else is watching?

Teach Me TORAH 4

WORDS TO KNOW

famous—well known

Humble—modest; not boastful

Babble—meaningless, confused words or sounds

Objectives

Students will be able to:

- Recognize the importance of language in bringing people together or keeping them apart
- Articulate the role humility plays in helping us recognize how we can effectively help others
- Distinguish between jobs that are impossible and those we can try to accomplish

Getting Started

Ask your students if they know someone who speaks a language other than English. How easy or difficult is it for them to understand that person? How many languages do your students think are spoken in the world? Take a poll, and write responses on the board. Ethnologue, a group categorizing the world's languages, now counts 6,912 spoken languages in the world. An Internet search of "world languages" will help you find examples for your students.

Using the Illustration

Have students find elements from the story. How are people working together to build the tower? *(Two are making bricks together; two are discussing the plan for the tower; a line of builders hand bricks to one another up the side of the tower.,)* How can they tell the tower is very tall? *(The top of it is in the clouds.)*

Overview

A key theme in the biblical account of the Tower of Babel is that people can be deluded by their own arrogance to turn their attention away from God and away from caring for each other. The builders of the tower want to be famous for their creation so they can brag about their powers. All other concerns become secondary. God confuses their language so they can no longer communicate, extinguishing their ability to collaborate and humbling them.

Core Concept

When we remember to be humble, we become mindful of what is within our control and what is beyond our human reach.

Teaching the Story

Q. Why does the story begin "Long ago the people of the earth had one language"? *(Many languages are spoken today.)*

Q. How were the people of the city behaving badly? *(They were bragging about becoming famous for their tower.)*

Q. What happened to the people? *(They all began to speak different languages; they could not understand each other; they could not work together.)*

Q. Why do you think the people moved away after work on the tower stopped? *(They wanted to find other people who spoke the same language.)*

Teach Me MORE Torah

Babel (or Bavel, in Hebrew) is the name used in the Bible for the ancient city of Babylon. There is evidence there of a ziggurat (a pyramid-shaped, stair-stepped tower) there that was destroyed by the Hittites in 1531 B.C.E. Ziggurats often had temples on their tops, a way of symbolically reaching to heaven.

The ancient word *bab-el* meant "gate of God" while the Hebrew word *balel* (or *balbel*) means "to confuse" hence, the pun of babel and babble works in both Hebrew and English.

"We will build a city," they said. "And a tower with its top in the heavens! We will be famous for it. We will live here always. People will remember us forever."

God came down and saw the tower they were building. "This is just the beginning of what they will try to do!" God said. The people thought the tower was more important than anything else.

So God changed the one language into many languages. The builders could not talk to each other. They could not make bricks together. They could not build the tower together.

And all the work stopped.

The tower was never finished. The people moved away. The empty city was called Babel. And so, even today, when people talk in a way no one can understand, we call it babble.

2

Using the Illustration

Ask the students how the illustration on page two is different from the one on the first page. *(No one is working on the tower; grass is growing on it—it looks abandoned; people are walking off in different directions; one person is walking off all alone; one person is helping another person walk—the only help people offer each other in the first illustration is help to make the tower.)*

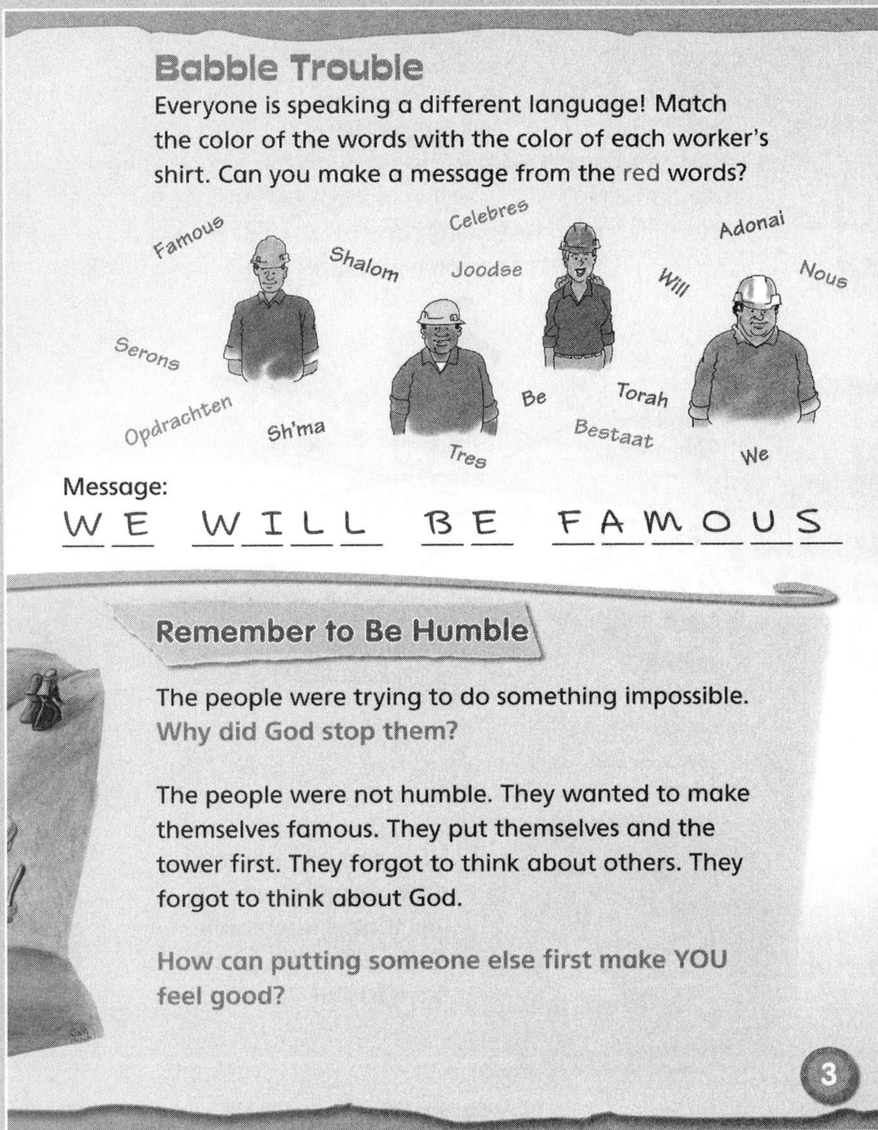

Babble Trouble

Everyone is speaking a different language! Match the color of the words with the color of each worker's shirt. Can you make a message from the red words?

Message:
WE WILL BE FAMOUS

Remember to Be Humble

The people were trying to do something impossible. Why did God stop them?

The people were not humble. They wanted to make themselves famous. They put themselves and the tower first. They forgot to think about others. They forgot to think about God.

How can putting someone else first make YOU feel good?

3

Bring the Story to Life: Babel Builders

There are many fun ways to get your class to think about the difficulties of communicating without language. You might have them try a simple game of charades, in teams. Or, you can bring in plastic building blocks, such as Legos,™ and have groups build their own Towers of Babel. Divide the class into teams, and have each team choose an "architect." Give each architect a "plan" for the group's tower. For example, one plan could show 18 blocks stacked in a pattern of two red, two blue, and two white repeated three times. Change patterns for each group. The architect must then get his or her group to correctly build the tower, without speaking, without touching any of the blocks, and without showing the group the plan.

Babble Trouble

Make this into a group or class activity by copying the colored words from the exercise onto large index cards. Hand out the index cards and have the students organize themselves into the correct groups. Have the whole class help the members of the red group form the mystery message: WE WILL BE FAMOUS.

Have fun with the other language cards as well. The blue cards are all Hebrew words. How many do your students recognize? (You may wish to write them in Hebrew as well as in transliteration). The green words are in French. The words in order *(nous serons tres celebres)* translate to "We will be very famous." The orange words are Dutch. *Joodse* (Jewish); *Opdrachten* (commands/mitzvot); *Bestaat* (has or exists). In 2001 the Behrman House book *My Jewish Year* was translated into Dutch: *Mijn Joodse Jaar.*)

My D'var Torah: Remember to Be Humble

Remind your students that extravagant gestures are not always the ones that mean the most. Ask students: What do you think was happening to the sick people when everyone in Babel was concentrating only on building a huge tower to make themselves famous? What was happening to those who could not take care of themselves?

Feel Tall

Have students discuss what the child in each vignette is doing. Is it really possible for us to save a person from a burning building by flying them out the window? What can we do that would work? *(Call the fire department; get help.)*

What is a better way to spend your time: finishing a job you can do well, or dreaming about doing the impossible? Which will have a better result?

Bring the Value to Life: Eitz Shel Todah (Thank You Tree)

Draw a tree trunk and branches on butcher paper, and cut out construction paper leaves. Ask students a broad question about who helps them accomplish a specific task. For example, who helps them play soccer? *(My coach; my sister who drives me to practice)* Write the names on the leaves and attach them to the tree.

Remind students that we are humble when we recognize that our success depends on other people's help—that our trees need help to bloom.

Feel Tall

You don't have to do the impossible to feel good. Even a small job, done well, can make us and others feel taller. Get to the top of the tower. Connect each brick to a job you can do well.

Ask at Home

How can you tell the difference between a job that is impossible and one that is just hard to do?

4

Ask at Home

Discuss the photo. Does everyone know how to tie his or her shoes? Tying shoes can be hard. What was it like to learn how to do it? What clues did you have that you would be able to do it? *(I know other people who can do it.)* Most people can learn how to tie a shoe. What are some things people cannot do? How do you know?

Abraham

Teach Me TORAH 5

Genesis 12:1-3
and 18:20–19:29

God chose Abraham to be the father of the Israelite people.

"Leave your home," God said. "Go to the land that I will show you. I will make you a great nation." So Abraham and his wife Sarah went to live in the land of Canaan. They followed God's ways.

But many people did not follow God's ways. God said, "I have heard that the cities of Sodom and Gomorrah are evil. If this is true, I will destroy them."

Overview

This folder presents elements of two Torah portions *(parashot): Lech Lecha* and *Va-yera*. In the first, we learn that God distinguishes Abraham by promising to make him "a great nation." In the second, we see elements of Abraham's suitability to become a patriarch. The story in this folder highlights Abraham's determination to understand God as just and merciful. Abraham negotiates with God to gain forgiveness even of evil people for the sake of innocent people. Abraham's deferential manner in undertaking this defense of the innocent underscores his fitness for the role God has given him.

Core Concept

We should speak up for others so that they are treated fairly and as we would wish to be treated.

Teach Me TORAH 5

WORDS TO KNOW

Nation—a group of people who share customs, origins, history, and often, language

Minyan—ten Jewish adults; the smallest number needed for a full prayer service

Objectives

Students will be able to:

- Identify Abraham as the father and Sarah as the mother of the Israelite people
- Discuss the importance of speaking up for others
- Identify and explain a *minyan*

Getting Started

Ask your students if any of them has ever moved to a new town or started attending a new school. What was it like to leave their old home or school and go someplace new and strange? Explain to students that the Torah tells us how Abraham and Sarah left the land of their families to go to Canaan and start a new life in the land God promised to them. When they arrived, they found people with customs and ways of living that were very different from their own.

Using the Illustration 1

Have students describe Abraham's expression. *(Sad, worried)* Who is the woman in the tent? *(Abraham's wife, Sarah)* Why is she important? (Background note: The rabbis counted 22 women in the Bible as "women of valor," from Proverbs 31:10. Of these, only Sarah was given an age in the Bible—127 years at her death. Thus, concluded the rabbis, Sarah is to be considered the greatest of all the women of the Bible.)

Ask students whom they think Abraham is talking to. (God) What clues can they find that might help them guess what Abraham is talking about? (His hand is pointing toward the two cities; Sarah—standing at the opening of the tent—is also looking at the cities.)

Teaching the Story

Q. **Abraham and Sarah followed God's ways. In the story, who did NOT follow God's ways?** *(The people of Sodom and Gomorrah.).*

Q. **The first time Abraham asked God to forgive the cities, how many good people would God need to find there?** *(50)*

Q. **The last time Abraham asked God to save the cities, how many good people had to be found?** *(Ten)*

Q. **How many good people did God find in Sodom and Gomorrah?** *(Not even ten; only Lot and his family were good.)*

Q. **Abraham asked God to forgive the cities for the sake of any good people living there. But God destroyed the cities. How do we know whether God listened to Abraham?** *(God burned Sodom and Gomorrah, but first God saved Lot and his family by warning them and telling them to escape. God knew Abraham did not want good people destroyed along with them, and so God saved Lot.)*

"But what if fifty good people are living there?" asked Abraham. "Will you kill good people as well as bad ones?"

"If I find fifty good people," God said. "I will let the cities stay."

"Please excuse me," said Abraham. "But perhaps there are only forty good people there, or only twenty. What then?" he asked.

"I will let the cities stay," said God.

"Please do not be angry if I speak again," said Abraham, "But what if you find only ten?"

"For the sake of ten good people the cities will be safe" said God.

But in all of Sodom and Gomorrah, there were not even ten good people. Only a man named Lot and his family were good. God called to Lot, "Run away! I will destroy these evil cities. Run away now, and do not look back!"

And then God burned Sodom and Gomorrah.

2

Teach Me MORE Torah

Abraham's name was originally Abram; Sarah's, Sarai. The Torah teaches that God added the Hebrew letter hey to their names. This hey represents the name of God and tradition teaches that Abraham and Sarah's new names carry with them a constant reference to the divine. It is after coming to Canaan, but before the destruction of Sodom and Gomorrah, that God changed their names (Genesis 17: 1-22). The Torah further tells us that God did this at the time of making a covenant with Abraham, promising that Abraham will be the father of many nations, promising a son to Sarah, and establishing circumcision as the sign of the covenant between God and Abraham.

Ten Good People

The Torah tells us that God agreed to save a whole city for the sake of ten good people. It takes ten Jews to make a ***minyan***, a group that prays together. Circle the groups that make a ***minyan***.

Standing Up for Others

Why did Abraham argue with God?

Sometimes we must speak up to help others. Abraham did not want good people to be destroyed, so he argued with God.

How does someone you know speak up for others?

3

Using the Illustration

What is happening to the cities? *(They are burning.)* God told Lot and his family to "run away and do not look back." Is there someone in the drawing who might not obey that command? *(The woman in the back)* What might she be thinking? *(That she does not want to leave her home; that she is afraid)* Can anyone guess who she is? *(Lot's wife)* Does anyone know what happens to her? *(She looks back and is turned into a pillar of salt.)* You might tell your class that today in the area surrounding the Dead Sea there is a geologic formation is known as "Lot's wife." An Internet search under "Lot's wife + images" will yield photos you may wish to share with your class.

Ten Good People

Have the students count the number of people in each group, and find the groups that make a minyan. Does anyone know what a minyan is? Explain that a minyan is the minimum number of Jewish adults required to hold a prayer service. The Jewish tradition of requiring a minyan for religious services comes in part from our sages' interpretation of this biblical passage.

You might point out to your students that for some Jews it is a custom to avoid directly counting people. It comes from folklore as a way to avoid the "evil eye." Thus, in some communities, a minyan might be counted by saying "Not 1, Not 2, Not 3 … " Ask students: what are some other ways we can count the students in our class? *(Give out index cards, then count the cards; have each student make a mark on the board, then count the marks.)* Be creative!

Bring the Story to Life: Argument Drama

Instruct students to find a partner and act out the conversation between God and Abraham. Pay careful attention to how the students playing Abraham and God make their opinions known. What tone do they use? How successful are their arguments? Explore these questions in a class discussion. Did the students playing Abraham bully the students playing God? Did they speak politely? You might also expand the conversation by asking, why did Abraham try to so hard to save the people of Sodom and Gomorrah? Why is it important for Jewish people to support all types of people, not just Jews?

My D'var Torah: Standing Up for Others

Encourage students to consider people from current events as well as people in the community who stand up for others.

They Need Your Help

Have students describe each scene. You may wish to have students take turns acting out each one.

Bring the Value to Life: Story Starters

Tell students that you are going to begin a story but that they will determine how it ends. Choose a story opener that will lead to a discussion that centers on the theme of standing up for others. Some examples include: *Hannah was smaller than Rachel. One day at lunch, Rachel took Hannah's cookie without asking ...* Or: *Madison and Ari were running a race. Another runner pushed Ari. He fell down. Madison looked at him and ...*

Begin the story and stop mid-sentence. Choose a student to continue the story and, after a time, pause him or her choose another student to continue the story. Continue until everyone has participated. Ask students, why is it important to stand up for others?

They Need Your Help!

Each picture below shows a person who needs someone to stand up for him or her. What can you say to help?

Ask at Home

Sometimes we get into arguments at home. How can you get someone to listen when you disagree?

4

 ISBN-10: 0-87441-825-9; ISBN-13: 978-0-87441-825-5.

Ask at Home

Ask students what they see happening in the photograph. What might these boys be fighting about? How well do you think they can listen to one another while they are pulling each other's hair? What happens when a disagreement ends in a fight? *(One person wins, one loses; both get into trouble; people get hurt.)* Have students brainstorm to find other, more effective strategies.

Genesis 24:1-67

Abraham wanted his son Isaac to marry.

So Abraham called to his servant. "Take ten camels and many gifts," he said. "Go back to the land I came from and find a wife for my son."

At a well in the center of one of the towns, the servant stopped. "When the girls of the town come for water, I will ask for a drink," he said. "The girl who offers water to me and to the camels will be the one God has chosen to be Isaac's wife."

Overview

After the death of his wife, Sarah, Abraham begins to plan for his own death by seeking to ensure the future of his house. He sends his servant back to his homeland in search of a wife for his son, Isaac. The servant looks, above all, for the quality of kindness, and in Rebecca finds a person whose generosity of spirit mirrors Abraham's own.

Core Concept

It is important to act kindly toward all of God's creatures, people and animals alike.

Objectives

Students will be able to:

- Identify ways in which Rebecca showed kindness
- Discuss the extent of Rebecca's good will, as shown by the size of the task she offers to complete
- List ways we can follow Rebecca's example

Teach Me TORAH 6

WORDS TO KNOW

Servant—a person hired to work in a household

Well—a deep hole dug to get water

Getting Started

Ask students to think of someone they would describe as kind. Tell them to put a picture of that person in their minds. Now ask them to think about some of the things that person does that show his or her kindness. Go around the room and ask students in turn about their person, and list their kindnesses on the board.

As an alternative, you can create "Kindness Awards." You can decorate adhesive-backed mailing labels (many come in sheets that will fit your computer's printer) that say KINDNESS AWARD given to _____ for _____.

Bring a large piece of colored poster board to class and label it "Kindness Awards." As you and your class complete the Getting Started activity, help each student fill out an award naming the person they are thinking of. Each student in turn can announce the name of the person and stick the label on the poster board.

You might also explain that in behaving the way they do, these people are demonstrating *derech eretz,* literally "the right road" which is the Jewish concept of behaving well, having good manners, and doing the right thing, including being kind. You may wish to continue having your students give out Kindness Awards as the year progresses.

Using the Illustration

Have students identify the characters in the story. Which one is Rebecca? Which one is the servant? Can they find the town? Is it close by or far away? When you are in your house, and want a drink of water, what do you do?

Compare what Rebecca had to do to get water for her family to how you get water. How will Rebecca get water for the camels? Does this seem like a small job or a big one?

Teaching the Story

Q. **Why did Abraham send his servant back to his homeland?** *(To find a wife for Isaac)*

Q. **How will the servant choose a wife for Isaac?** *(Someone who offers water to him and to his camels)*

Q. **What will offering water prove about this girl?** *(That she is extremely kind and generous)*

Q. **What other things does Rebecca offer to the servant?** *(She says her family has a place where the servant and the camels can stay, and offers straw for the camels.)*

Teach Me MORE Torah

The servant is not named in this chapter of Genesis. The traditional interpretation is that the servant is Eliezer, who is named in Genesis 15:2 as the one in charge of Abraham's household. Even Rashi, in his commentary about this chapter of Genesis assumed the servant was Eliezer (Rashi on Genesis 24:42).

The gifts Eliezer brought to give to the wife he chose for Isaac were two gold bracelets and a gold nose ring (Genesis 24:22).

Rebecca came to the well with her water jug. "Will you please give me a sip of the water from your jug?" the servant asked her.

Rebecca hurried over. "Please, sir, drink as much as you want," she said. "And let me get water for all your camels, too," she added.

"Is there a place I can stay for the night?" the servant asked.

"My family has room for a guest, and plenty of straw for the camels," said the girl. "My name is Rebecca."

"Such a kind girl will be a good wife for Isaac," the servant said to himself.

The servant gave Rebecca gifts—a gold ring and two gold bracelets. He asked her family if she would marry Isaac. "I will," said Rebecca. And she did.

2

Thirsty Camels

Help Rebecca get water for the camels.

Draw a line from each camel to a water jug. Does Rebecca have enough? Circle the number of water jugs Rebecca still needs to fill. 0 (1) 2

Showing Kindness

What made Abraham's servant decide that Rebecca would be a good wife for Isaac?

Rebecca gave water to the servant right away. She also took care of the animals without being asked. In this way, Rebecca showed that she was more than just polite. She showed she was kind.

How can **you** show kindness?

3

Using the Illustration

Ask students to compare the size of the watering trough to the size of the jug Rebecca is holding. Rebecca got water from a well. Ask students if they have ever seen an old- fashioned well. How did it work? How hard do they think it would be to fill up the trough in the illustration?

Thirsty Camels

This exercise suggests it took one jar of water for each camel. But just how kind was Rebecca? Well, let's think about what we know about camels. A camel can drink 25 gallons of water in 10 minutes. You can bring a gallon jug or two to class and have students see how long it takes to fill and bring back to class.

To make the trip even more like Rebecca's, have a madrich accompany the students to the water source that is the farthest from the classroom. What if Rebecca had to do this 25 times for each camel? Have your students figure out how many jugs of water that would be.

Bring the Story to Life: Welcoming Guests

Rebecca was kind to Abraham's servant, a visitor to her town and her family's guest. We also can be kind by welcoming new people in our class. Let students choose someone they would like to invite to class—perhaps a new cantor or teacher?

Before the guest arrives, help students prepare welcome signs and spend time brainstorming ways to make the visitor feel welcome. After the guest leaves, ask the class, how were you kind to our guest like Rebecca was kind to Abraham's servant?

My D'var Torah: Showing Kindness

Point out to your students that Rebecca, like Abraham, showed exceptional caring for others. In this way, she made an especially good choice to be Isaac's wife.

Seen at the Well

Have students point out and describe the behaviors they see. *(A person giving water to a camel; a person helping fill another's bucket; someone grabbing another's bucket away; one person pushing another away from the well.)*

Bring the Value to Life: Seeing Kindness

Bring magazines to class. Tell students to look through the magazines and find pictures of people who are being kind; for example, have them find an advertisement in which someone is feeding an animal or giving someone else a hug. Ask each student to describe the picture he or she has chosen and how it shows kindness.

Seen At the Well

Not everyone at the well is as kind as Rebecca. Cross out those who are not acting kindly. Color the ones who are.

Ask at Home

What does kindness look like to you?

4

Ask at Home

Ask students: What happened just before this picture was taken? How do you think the little boy was feeling? What feelings do you think he is having now that someone is taking care of him? Is there something special that someone does for you? How does it make you feel? Explain that kindness can feel differently to each of us. We have to put ourselves in others' places to understand what we can do to be kind to them.

Genesis 25:19–27:45
and 32:4–33:17

Isaac and Rebecca had twin sons named Jacob and Esau. The boys did not get along.

Even before they were born, Jacob and Esau fought to be first. The first to be born would have a birthright. He would become leader of the family. The first to be born was Esau.

As the brothers grew older, they still fought to be first. One day Esau returned from hunting and saw Jacob making soup. "I'm starving!" said Esau. "Give me that red stuff!"

Overview

Isaac and Rebecca have twin sons, Esau and Jacob, who could not be more different. Their differences lead to lifelong conflict and tension between the two. Ultimately, Jacobs tricks his brother out of the blessing and the inheritance that typically belongs to the firstborn son. Only many years later do Jacob and Esau agree to put aside their differences and go their separate ways in peace.

Core Concept

We should respect and value our family members in order to bring about *sh'lom bayit*—peace in our homes and with our families.

Objectives

Students will be able to:

- Describe the conflicts between Jacob and Esau
- Discuss the importance of resolving conflicts with our family members

Teach Me TORAH

7

WORDS TO KNOW

Birthright—privileges traditionally given to the oldest son, including the right to lead the family and inherit a larger share of the family's belongings

Getting Started

Even though people belong to the same family, they can be very different. Before reading the story, ask your students to describe how they are like their siblings or others in their families, and how they are different. When do these differences make it hard to get along? Then set the scene for this vivid story of Jacob and Esau by describing two brothers who are very different—one has red hair and very hairy arms and legs; one has dark hair and smooth skin. One is athletic, and likes to be outdoors, hunting with a bow and arrow; the other likes to stay close to home, and often helps by cooking. One is loud; the other is quiet. They are so different that they have a hard time getting along. The father likes the hunter best; the mother likes the quiet boy best.

Using the Illustration

Ask what color they see the most in this illustration. How does it make them feel?

Ask if they have ever heard the expression "I am so angry I see red." Red is often seen as the color of anger. Which brother do they think is Esau? *(Esau is on the left, in the blue tunic.)* Which one is Jacob? *(Jacob is on the right in the green tunic.)* What color is Esau's hair? *(Red)* Would they describe Esau as an angry person? Why or why not? What about Jacob?

Teaching the Story

Q. **Who was born first?** *(Esau)* **Who was born second?** *(Jacob)*

Q. **Why did Esau sell his birthright to Jacob?** *(He was hungry and wanted the stew that Jacob had cooked.)*

Q. **How important was Esau's birthright and inheritance to him?** *(Not very important—he was willing to give it away to get some dinner.)*

Q. **What else did Jacob get that was meant for Esau?** *(Jacob tricked his father into giving him Esau's blessing as the oldest son. He got the right to lead the family.)*

Q. **Why did Jacob run away?** *(Esau was going to kill him for taking his birthright and his blessing.)*

Q. **How were Jacob and Esau able to make peace with each other?** *(Jacob sent gifts to Esau and bowed before him; Esau ran to meet Jacob when he returned, hugged him, and told him to keep what was his. They each treated the other with respect.)*

Q. **Do you think Jacob and Esau finally became friends as well as brothers?** *(Perhaps yes, perhaps no; the Torah tells us they went their separate ways in peace.)*

"Sell me your birthright first," Jacob said. Esau did not care about his birthright. So he sold his rights as the oldest son for a pot of lentil soup.

When their father Isaac grew very old, Jacob pretended to be Esau, and tricked Isaac to get the blessing promised to his brother.

Now Jacob, not Esau, had his father's blessing to lead the family.

Esau was furious. "Jacob took my birthright and my blessing," he wailed. "When my father dies, I will kill him to get what belongs to me."

So Jacob ran away. He was gone many years.

When Jacob came back, he was still afraid of Esau. So he sent gifts to his brother. When he saw Esau, Jacob bowed seven times. When Esau saw his brother, he ran to meet him and hugged him. "I have plenty," Esau said. "Keep what is yours."

And then Jacob and Esau went their separate ways in peace.

2

Teach Me MORE Torah

Before the birth of Jacob and Esau, the Torah tells us that Rebecca received the message that "the older will serve the younger" (Genesis 25:23). In addition, the rabbis have pointed out that Esau's manner—his uncouth speech, and his impulsiveness in selling his birthright for stew suggests that he would not make a suitable leader of the nation God promised to Abraham and his progeny.

On the night before Jacob is to meet Esau for the first time since he ran away, Jacob wrestles with a *malakh,* which is Hebrew for "messenger." The Greek word for messenger is *angelos,* from which we get the English word "angel." Thus, we talk of Jacob wrestling with an angel. The angel changes Jacob's name to Israel, which means "he who wrestles with God" (Genesis 32:29). This is why Jacob's descendents became known as the Israelites.

What's Important?

Complete the picture: what was more important to Esau than his own birthright?

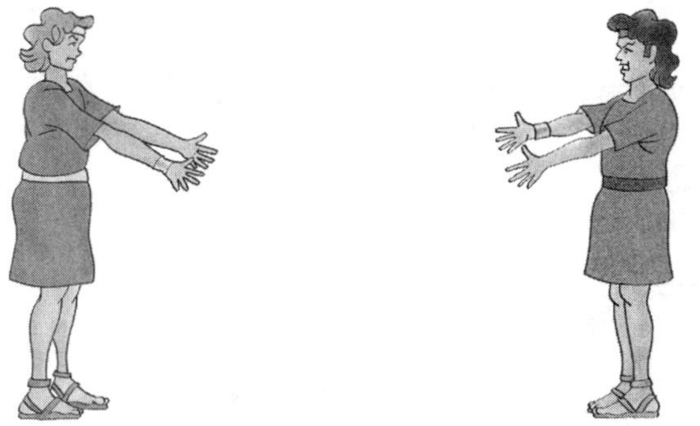

Keeping Peace in Your Family

After years of treating each other badly, how were Jacob and Esau finally able to make peace?

Each brother treated the other with respect and care. Jacob sent gifts. He bowed to his older brother as a sign of respect. Esau ran to Jacob, and hugged him. He told Jacob he wanted nothing.

How can you help keep peace at home?

3

Using the Illustration

Which man is Esau and which is Jacob? What is Jacob doing? Why do you think this might help the brothers get along?

What's Important?

Ask your students: Does it make sense to fight over a bowl of stew? If lentil stew does not sound very appetizing, would they feel differently if it was a pizza? How important do you think his birthright was to Esau?

Bring the Story to Life: Who Deserves the Birthright?

Divide the class into two groups: one that wants Jacob to receive the birthright and one that wants Esau to receive it. Take turns asking each group for reasons why their brother should get the birthright. Record their answers on the board. Those supporting Jacob might say that he bought the birthright fairly and was less violent. Those supporting Esau might counter that he was older and was cheated.

My D'var Torah: Keeping Peace in Your Family

Read the opening question and have students consider answers before reading the lesson. Follow with the second question and solicit student answers for ways they can think of to keep the peace at home. You might ask students for examples of belongings or activities that family members fight over and ask them what they might do to avoid these kinds of arguments.

You can have students complete the "Keep the Peace" activity on page four individually, work in small groups, or discuss it as a class. Have students describe what is happening in each picture and why it does or does not show respect.

Bonus Activity: students can work in groups or you can have students call out the letters and write them on the board to spell SHALOM, the Hebrew word for PEACE.

Bring the Value to Life: *Sh'lom Bayit*

Before class, draw an outline of a house on a piece of paper and label it, "*Sh'lom Bayit* Contract." Include two signature lines, one for the student and one for a parent. Make photocopies of the contract.

During class, tell students that shalom means "peace" and *bayit* is Hebrew for "home," so *sh'lom bayit* means "peace in the home." (The Hebrew is written a little differently when the two words are combined, so the transliteration changes slightly as well.)

Ask students how they bring peace into their homes. Do they share their toys with siblings? Do they clean their rooms? Explain that a contract is something we sign when we agree to do something. Ask them, do you agree to try to bring peace into your homes?

Distribute the *sh'lom bayit* contracts to the students to be decorated with the people and things that bring peace to their homes. Have the students sign the contract, and send it home for their parents to sign as well.

Ask at Home

Tell your students that it is customary for parents to bless their children on Shabbat. In the blessings, parents ask God to make their daughters like Sarah, Rebecca, Rachel and Leah. They ask God to make their sons like Ephraim and Manasseh.

Students may be able at this point to identify Sarah (Abraham's wife, mother of Isaac), and Rebecca (the kind girl found at the well who became Isaac's wife and the mother of Jacob and Esau). Explain that Rachel and Leah were sisters, and became Jacob's wives. Rachel was Joseph's mother.

Students are less likely to know Ephraim and Manasseh, Joseph's sons. They are admired because, unlike Jacob and Esau, Ephraim and Manasseh were not known to be jealous of one another, even though Ephraim—the younger—was blessed by their grandfather Jacob as the brother who would become greater than his older brother (Genesis 48:20). Moses was a descendent of Ephraim's.

Complete Shabbat blessings for parents are available on the family pages at www.behrmanhouse.com. You may wish to print them out and send them home along with the Jacob and Esau folder.

Joseph

Genesis 37:1–47:27

Jacob had twelve sons. Joseph was his favorite. This made the other eleven furious.

They hated Joseph. They hated the colorful coat their father had given him. They even hated Joseph's dreams. "In my dreams," Joseph said, "you all bow down to me."

The brothers did not want to bow to Joseph. They would not even speak nicely to him. They wanted to get rid of him.

Overview

Sibling rivalry—fueled by parents favoring one child over another—is again a central theme in the story of Joseph. This story ends with the Israelites leaving Canaan for Egypt, setting the stage for their eventual enslavement. Year after they sell their own brother into slavery, famine forces Jacob's other sons to travel to Egypt. There, they are recognized by Joseph, who tests them and finds that they are sorry for their earlier rash action. Finally, the family reconciles.

Core Concept

Asking for forgiveness and admitting our mistakes is hard, but apologizing helps us bring peace into our lives.

Objectives

Students will be able to:

- Identify Joseph as Jacob's son and name some of his brothers
- Describe the harmful effects of jealousy and boasting
- Discuss ways to forgive people who have hurt us
- Explain how the Israelites came to settle in Egypt

Teach Me TORAH 8

WORDS TO KNOW

Jealousy—a resentful or bitter feeling of competition

Forgiveness—a decision to accept an apology

Getting Started

Bring a box or two of doughnut holes to class. Begin by placing all the treats in front of one student. Ask the class: "What if I decided to choose one of you as my favorite student, and gave just that child a special treat?"

Have the class discuss the possible results if you were to do this. How would the other students feel? What would coming to class be like for the favorite student? For the non-favorites? What would be a better way for you to treat the students in the class? End your discussion by having the students decide how to distribute the doughnut holes fairly.

Using the Illustration

Point out Joseph; how is he dressed differently than his brothers? Can they find Jacob? Look at the brothers on the left; what do you think they are saying to one another? What do you think is about to happen next?

Teaching the Story

Q. **Who was Jacob's favorite son?** *(Joseph)*

Q. **What gift did Joseph receive from his father?** *(A colorful coat)*

Q. **What made Joseph's brothers so angry with him?** *(Joseph got a fancy gift from their father and Joseph bragged about his dream that all the other brothers would bow down to him.)*

Q. **How do we know the brothers were angry with Joseph?** *(They would not even speak nicely to Joseph.)*

Q. **How do you think Joseph felt about his brothers at the beginning of the story? At the end?**

Teach Me MORE Torah 1

Joseph was the firstborn son of Jacob's favorite wife, Rachel. This is the reason most often given for Joseph's special place in his father's heart. Rachel's only other son was Benjamin, the youngest. All of Jacob's other sons were half-brothers of Joseph.

Before telling his brothers to come live with him in Egypt, Joseph tests them. He first accuses them of being spies, and then of stealing from him. Only after Judah offers himself as a slave in order to save Benjamin does Joseph relent and reveal himself to the brothers (Genesis 44-45).

So the brothers sold Joseph and he was taken to Egypt as a slave. They put goat's blood on Joseph's coat and took it to their father. "A wild animal ate him!" cried Jacob. And he wept for his son.

Joseph lived in Egypt many years. He helped Pharaoh, the king of Egypt, save the Egyptians from terrible hunger at a time when no food would grow.

Joseph's brothers were also hungry. They came to Egypt to ask for food. After so many years, they did not recognize Joseph. He looked and dressed like an Egyptian. But Joseph knew them. "How many brothers do you have?" he asked.

"Our father had twelve sons, but one is gone. It is our fault. We are sorry," they answered.

"Do not be upset," Joseph told them. "I am your brother! I know God sent me here to save our lives. You must all come live in Egypt with me."

And that is how the Children of Israel came to live in the land of Egypt.

2

Teach Me MORE Torah 2

Jacob not only caused envy among his sons by his lavish treatment of Joseph, but he also seemed to allow Joseph to spy on his brothers. "And Joseph brought bad reports of them to his father" (Genesis 37:2). In the Babylonian Talmud (Shabbat 10b), the rabbis warn of the dire consequences when a parent favors one child over others, citing Jacob's preferential treatment of Joseph as eventually leading to the Israelites becoming slaves in Egypt.

Using the Illustration 2

Compare this picture of Joseph to the one on the first page. Why might Joseph's brothers not recognize him? Count the brothers. What are they doing? Did Joseph's dream come true?

In His Dreams

Complete the picture to show Joseph's dream about his brothers. Don't forget Joseph's **colorful coat!**

Asking for Forgiveness

What helped Joseph and his brothers get along again?

Joseph's brothers told him how sorry they were. Joseph also realized that he was sent to Egypt with a purpose—to save the lives of his family and many others. He felt he was sent by God.

What helps you forgive someone who has been mean to you?

3

In His Dreams

You can have students re-enact the dream rather than draw it. Bring in a colorful afghan or shawl to be Joseph's coat. Have other students be the brothers. Ask students: what does it mean to bow to others? *(Although it is traditional in some cultures, such as the Japanese, for people to bow to each other as a sign of respect, bowing is usually considered a sign of subservience or inequality.)*

Bring the Story to Life: Colorful Coats

Ask students to each bring in a plain white T-shirt to class. Distribute fabric pens and let the children be creative. While the children decorate their shirts, consider playing songs from Andrew Lloyd Webber and Tim Rice's musical, *Joseph and the Amazing Technicolor Dreamcoat.* Challenge the students to identify the colors in the song "Joseph's Coat." Some of the hardest include: ochre (light yellow-brown), azure (blue), and russet (brown with reddish tinge).

You also can bring in a box of 64 Crayola™ Crayons. Have the students pass around the box and choose unusual colors to complete the activity on page three of the folder. Ask them to see if they can find colors mentioned in the song.

Extra fun: Play "Bingo Brothers" to help your class learn the names of the brothers and the twelve tribes. Use small poster board to create bingo cards, each with nine squares (like a tic-tac-toe board). Write one name in each square. Use a different mix of names and positions on each card. Hand out the cards, and give your students pennies or plastic game pieces. Have a student or madrich pull names from a bowl, one at a time, and read them out loud. The first student to get three in a row in any direction wins. This game is fast, so repeats are easy and create numerous winners.

My D'var Torah: Asking for Forgiveness

Remind students that in the days leading up to Yom Kippur we ask others to forgive us for wrongs we have done them. We have to seek forgiveness from other people before we seek forgiveness from God.

Forgive Me

Students may work individually, or you can divide the class into groups to collaborate. You can also complete the activity together as a class, by having students call out the red letters in turn and then writing them on the board to complete the mystery sentence (I AM SORRY).

To make this activity even more interactive, copy each brother's name onto a piece of poster board, making the red letters extra large and bold. Hand out one card per student, and then call up each "brother" in turn to form the sentence. Students who have cards with no red letters can be the "spaces" between the words created from the red letters. NOTE: be sure to make a red Y to complete the sentence!

Bring the Value to Life: *Slichah*

Ask the class how it feels to say "I'm sorry." Teach the class the Hebrew word *sliḥah.* Jewish tradition teaches us the importance of *sliḥah*—apologizing and asking forgiveness. Encourage the children to say *sliḥah* when they apologize.

One way to expand this activity is by teaching students to say "I'm sorry" in sign language. Search online for "sign language + sorry" for instructions. Remind students that there are many ways to say "I'm sorry" with different languages and gestures. Ask your students if they can think of actions that show "I'm sorry."

Forgive Me

Copy the red letters from the names of Joseph's brothers onto the lines below to spell out the secret message that helped them all get along again.

LEVI NAPTHALI ZEBULUN

JUDAH BENJAMIN ASHER

SIMEON REUBEN DAN

GAD ISSACHAR

I A M S O R R Y

Ask at Home

When someone else gets a gift, it can be hard not to feel jealous. What can you think about to feel better?

4

Ask at Home

Can the students tell a story about what has just happened in the photograph? *(Perhaps it is a birthday party and the boy just got a gift.)* How do think the girl in the pink dress feels? What do you think she is thinking? (She might wish she was getting a gift. She can think about when it will be her turn to have a birthday.)

Teach Me TORAH 9

Miriam and Moses

Exodus 1:1–2:10

Egypt was filled with the Children of Israel. Pharaoh made all of them slaves.

But this was not enough for Pharaoh. "In a war they might join our enemies and fight against us," he said.

Pharaoh ordered two Hebrew midwives to kill all the baby Israelite boys as they were born. But the women let the babies live. So Pharaoh turned to his own people. "Throw them into the river!" he commanded the Egyptians.

Overview

Pharaoh fears the Jewish slaves and commands that Jewish baby boys be killed. But not everyone listens. The midwives would not let Jewish baby boys be hurt, and Moses' sister Miriam, his mother, and Pharaoh's daughter helped him to survive.

Core Concept

In our own lives, we can choose how we allow others to be treated. We can watch while people or family members get hurt, or we can try to help others lead happy and healthy lives.

Objectives

Students will be able to:

- Name the ruler of Egypt *(Pharaoh),* Moses, and Moses' sister *(Miriam).*
- Identify the women who helped save Moses' life
- Recount how Moses' family worked together to ensure his safety
- Describe people we know today who work hard to protect our lives

WORDS TO KNOW

Pharaoh—the ruler of Egypt

The Israelites—descendants of Jacob; later, the Jewish people

Midwife—someone who helps a woman give birth

Getting Started

Bring in a baby doll to class. Ask the student what this baby needs to be happy and healthy. *(Nurturing parents; good food; a place to live)*

Ask students to think of something they could do to help protect the baby, such as covering the baby with a blanket or protecting the baby from rain. Remind students that babies need a lot of help and love from a lot of people. Tell students that many people helped Moses to survive when he was a baby.

Using the Illustration

After reading through the story, have students turn back to the first page. Can they find elements from the story? Where is baby Moses? *(In the basket floating in the Nile)* Who watches over Moses? *(Miriam—Moses' sister)* Who is reaching out to Moses? *(Pharaoh's daughter)*

Teaching the Story

Q. **Where were the Children of Israel living?** *(Egypt)*

Q. **Why did the ruler of Egypt make the Israelites slaves?** *(Pharaoh was scared that the Israelites would fight against him.)*

Q. **What did Pharaoh command be done to Israelite baby boys?** *(Pharaoh commanded that Jewish midwives kill all Israelite baby boys. Then, he commanded that all Israelite baby boys be thrown in the Nile River.)*

Q. **What did Moses' mother do to save Moses?** *(She placed him in a basket. She placed the basket in the Nile River. Then, she told Miriam, Moses' sister, to watch the basket.)*

Q. **Who found Moses in the basket floating in the Nile?** *(Pharaoh's daughter)*

Q. **How did Miriam help Pharaoh's daughter?** *(Miriam found someone to take care of Moses—his own mother!)*

One mother had a plan to save her son. She smeared sticky tar all over a basket so it would not leak. Then she put her baby in the basket, and hid it among the reeds near the shore of the river.

"Watch the basket," she told her daughter, Miriam. So Miriam watched. Miriam saw Pharaoh's daughter come to bathe in the river. She watched the princess discover the basket.

"This must be a Hebrew baby!" the princess cried when she opened the basket. And she took pity on the crying baby.

Miriam came forward out of the reeds. "I know a woman who can nurse the baby," Miriam told the princess. And she brought the baby's own mother to care for him.

When the boy grew, the princess made him her son, and named him Moses. "For I pulled him out of the water," she said. And so Moses, the Hebrew baby, became the son of an Egyptian princess.

2

Teach Me MORE Torah

What's in a name? Many names in the Bible reflect the characteristics or circumstances of the people who bear them. As we learn in this story, Moses' name is connected to the Hebrew root which means "to draw out of water." Why did Pharaoh's daughter give him a Hebrew name when she was Egyptian? Perhaps to acknowledge Moses' origins.

Although her name is not mentioned in the Torah, our sages teach us that Pharaoh's daughter was named "Bitya," meaning "daughter of God" in Hebrew. Her actions reflect her humanity and forever connect her to the history of the Jewish people.

Two other significant names include the name of the Hebrew midwives who refused to kill Israelite baby boys: Shifrah and Puah. "Shifrah" comes from the Hebrew root meaning "beauty" and "Puah" is related to an ancient word meaning "young girl."

Save Moses

Circle the people who helped save baby Moses.

Protecting Life

Who really saved baby Moses?

It took many people to save baby Moses. The Hebrew midwives refused to follow Pharaoh's orders. Moses' mother hid him in a basket by the river. Miriam watched over the baby. Pharaoh's own daughter drew the baby from the water to keep as her own.

Name someone you know who protects life.

3

Using the Illustration 2

Ask students to describe what is happening. Who is holding baby Moses? *(Pharaoh's daughter)* Who is peeking out from behind the reeds? *(Miriam)* Why might she be hiding? *(Perhaps she does not want Pharaoh's daughter to see her.)* Why is Miriam happy? (*Baby Moses has been saved.)*

Save Moses

Have students as a class point to people who helped save baby Moses. Ask students also to point out the person who did not help save Moses.

Bring the Story to Life: Women of the Bible

Ask students to name all the biblical characters they know. Most names will probably be male. Remind students that there are many famous women, such as Moses' sister—Miriam; his mother, Yocheved; and Pharaoh's daughter, whom Jewish tradition calls Bitya.

Let students write thank you cards to these biblical heroines. Encourage them to thank the characters for specific actions *(Thank you, Miriam, for watching over your brother)*. Display the cards in the classroom. You may wish to extend this activity by letting students write thank you cards to Jewish women (or men) in their own lives.

My D'var Torah: Protecting Life

Ask students how the people they name protect life and keep others safe. How are their actions similar to those of the people who saved Moses?

It's a Match

Have students turn to the back page of the folder. Did they name any of the people on the page? Which ones? Then, let students complete the exercise and connect each person to his or her occupational tool.

To finish, ask students to answer the question about the tzedakah box. Be sure to have a tzedakah box and some coins handy. Let students practice placing coins in the box to begin their own efforts to protect life.

Bring the Value to Life: Blanket Drive

Tzedakah comes in many forms. One way to give tzedakah is to collect blankets to donate to local shelters. Enlist parents' help by sending home a letter announcing the drive. To remind students of the blanket drive, create a class quilt to hang in the classroom.

One way to make a class quilt is to have students write their names on cloth squares. Glue the squares on a large piece of poster board and hang it in class. Alternatively, if possible, ask a parent to sew the fabric squares into a quilt.

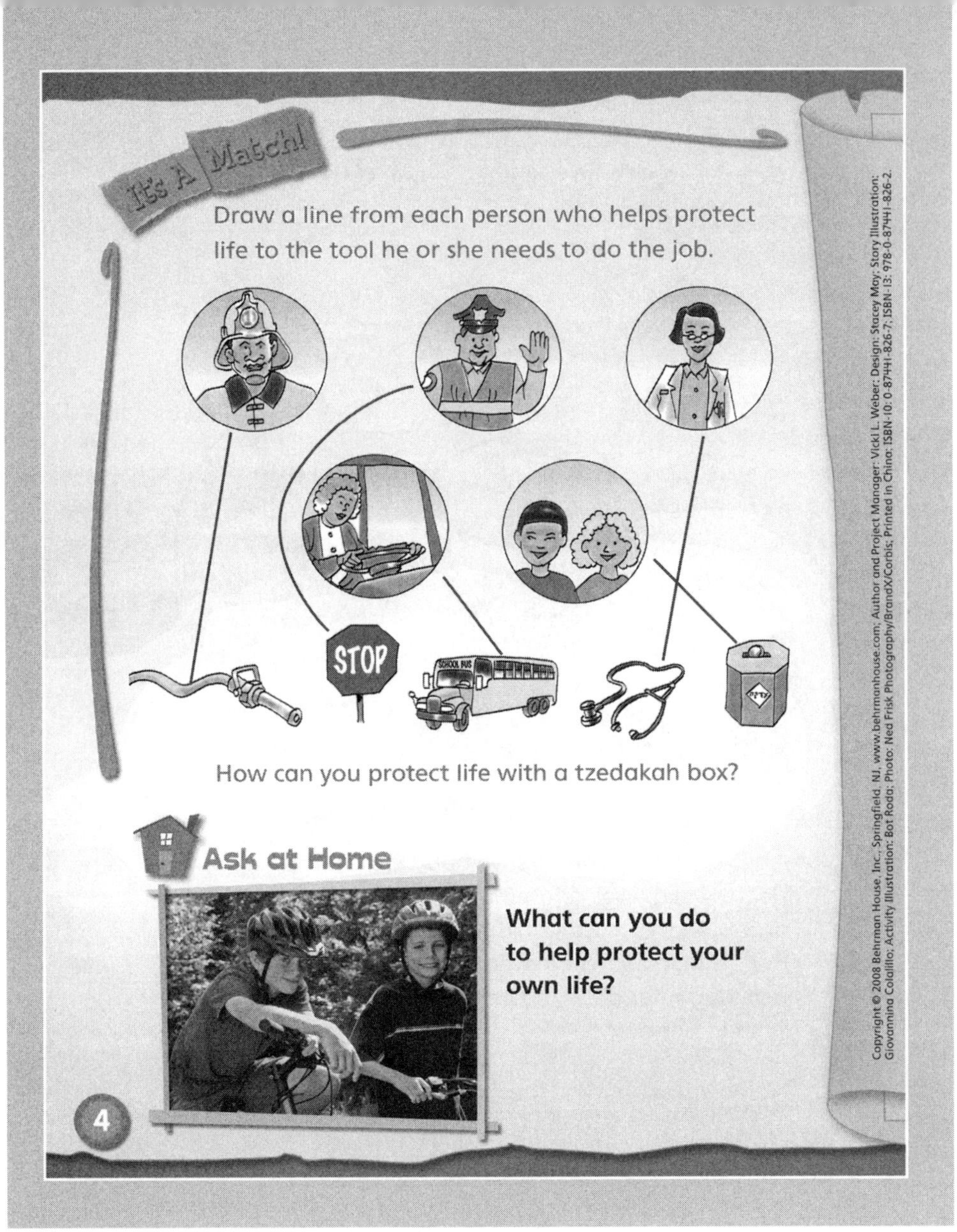
It's A Match!

Draw a line from each person who helps protect life to the tool he or she needs to do the job.

How can you protect life with a tzedakah box?

Ask at Home

What can you do to help protect your own life?

4

Ask at Home

How do the boys in the photograph protect themselves? *(They wear helmets.)* Explain that some ways we can protect ourselves include eating healthfully, getting a good night's sleep, and making good friends. Begin a discussion by asking students, how do you protect your own life when you are at home? How do your family members help?

Moses left Egypt, but God told him to go back. "Go tell Pharaoh to let my people go."

So Moses went back to Egypt. "The God of Israel commands 'Let my people go,'" he said to Pharaoh.

"NO!" said Pharaoh.

God sent plagues that tormented the Egyptians. After each plague Moses said, "Let my people go."

"NO!" said Pharaoh.

Teach Me TORAH 10

Overview

The Exodus story is about trust. Moses trusts in God and becomes the leader of the Children of Israel. Pharaoh does not trust in God and Egypt is punished with ten plagues. The Children of Israel trust in God and walk to safety and freedom through the parted Sea of Reeds.

Core Concept

Trusting in God helps us through difficult times and maintains the Jewish people.

Objectives

Students will be able to:

- Tell the story of the Israelites' exodus from Egypt
- Name two plagues that God sent against the Egyptians
- Explain how trusting in God helped saved the Children of Israel from slavery
- Distinguish between trusting in God, trusting each other, and trusting ourselves

WORDS TO KNOW

Plague—an evil punishment

Exodus—although not in the folder, "Exodus" refers to the Israelites' flight from Egypt as well as a biblical book and parsha.

Getting Started

Create a role play. You are Pharaoh and your students are the Children of Israel. Tell your students that they must try to convince you to let you go free. No matter what they say, respond, "no."

When they begin to become frustrated, ask them who might be able to convince you to let them go. *(Moses, God)* Tell students that the Israelites were only able to leave Egypt because they placed their trust in God and God's servant, Moses.

Using the Illustration

After reading through the story, have students turn back to the first page. Who is speaking to Pharaoh? (Moses) What is Moses asking? *("Let my people go.")* What does the way Pharaoh is standing tell us about him? *(He is stubborn; he doesn't believe Moses' claim that God will punish Egypt)*

Finally God sent a plague that killed the first-born son of every Egyptian family. Not a single house lay untouched by death. A loud cry went up in Egypt, and Pharaoh called for Moses.

"Take the people and GO!" cried Pharaoh.

The Israelites rushed to leave Egypt. They grabbed up their unbaked bread before the dough even had time to rise, and followed Moses.

But Pharaoh changed his mind. His army chased the Israelites to the Sea of Reeds. The Israelites were terrified. "It was better for us to be slaves in Egypt than to die in the wilderness!" they cried.

"See what God will do," said Moses.

Moses stretched his hand out over the water. It split apart and the Israelites crossed to the other side.

The Egyptians tried to follow. The water came crashing down and swept Pharaoh's army away.

When the Israelites saw the powers God had used to save them from Egypt, they trusted in God, and in their leader, Moses.

2

Teaching the Story

Q. **Who chose Moses to lead the Israelites out of Egypt?** *(God)*

Q. **What did Moses say to Pharaoh?** *(Let my people go.)*

Q. **What did Pharaoh respond to Moses?** *(No)*

Q. **What finally made Pharaoh free the Israelites?** *(The tenth plague: death of the firstborn)*

Q. **What did Pharaoh do after the Israelites left?** *(He changed his mind. The Egyptian army chased after the Israelites.)*

Q. **How did the Israelites react?** *(They were scared and cried out that it might be better for them to have remained slaves.)*

Q. **How were the Israelites saved?** *(Moses stretched his hand over the Sea of Reeds and God split the sea. The people walked to safety and trusted in God.)*

Teach Me MORE Torah

Was Moses the only Jewish leader? Did he have help? In fact, Moses had a brother, Aaron, who was three years older than Moses. He also had an older sister, Miriam. (She was old enough to watch over Moses when he was an infant in the basket.) Both Aaron and Miriam held leadership roles in the exodus from Egypt.

Tradition teaches us that Moses was a stutterer. When charged with the task to appear before Pharaoh, Moses hesitated. God reassured him by saying that Aaron would accompany Moses and would speak on his behalf (Exodus 4:10-16).

Miriam also was a leader among the Israelites, especially the women. After the Israelites walked across the Sea of Reeds to freedom and safety, Miriam led them in a song of praise and thanks to God (Exodus 15:20). She played the timbrel, a kind of drum.

Using the Illustration 2

Ask students to describe what is happening. What is Moses holding out over the sea? *(His staff—a wooden rod)* What are the women looking at? *(Pharaoh's army approaching)* Ask students, why are the women not watching Moses? *(They were scared and confused.)*

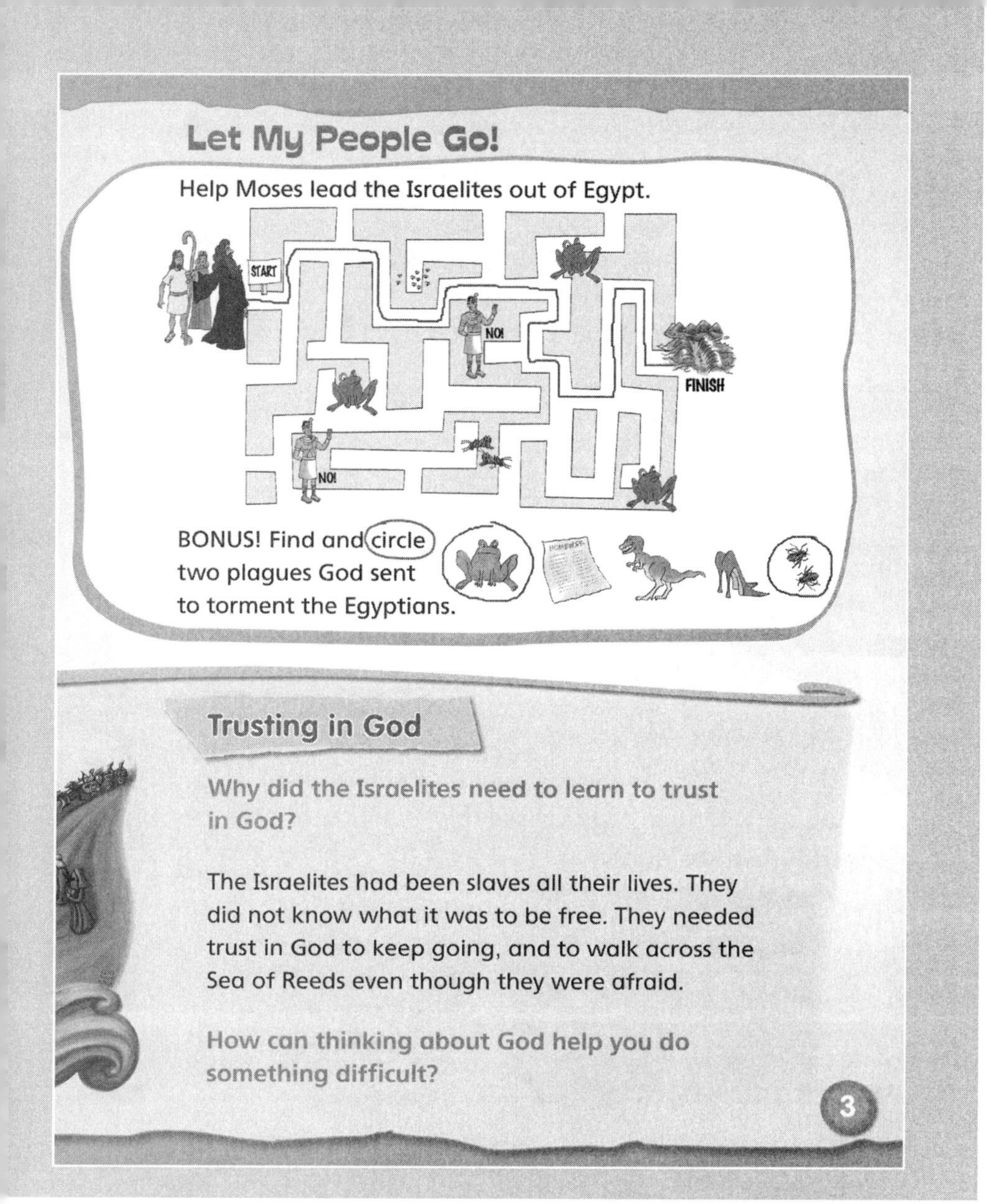

Let My People Go!

Help Moses lead the Israelites out of Egypt.

BONUS! Find and circle two plagues God sent to torment the Egyptians.

Trusting in God

Why did the Israelites need to learn to trust in God?

The Israelites had been slaves all their lives. They did not know what it was to be free. They needed trust in God to keep going, and to walk across the Sea of Reeds even though they were afraid.

How can thinking about God help you do something difficult?

3

Let My People Go

Have students complete the maze. Consider timing them. When students finish the maze, ask them if the plagues God sent also delayed the Israelites' exodus. Notice that in the maze, the plagues are large and disruptive. Pharaoh's stubbornness, which caused God to send plagues, did cause the Israelites' exodus to take longer.

Bring the Story to Life: Re-enacting the Exodus

Let students re-enact the Israelite's exodus from Egypt. Announce that today is a great day, because Pharaoh has agreed to let them—the Israelite slaves—leave Egypt. Tell students to rush around and collect their belongings. Then, they must hurry out of Egypt. Instruct them to file out of classroom and lead them on a journey through building. Let them cross the Sea of Reeds by gathering students together in front of blue poster board and encouraging them to raise their arms high, just as Moses did. Announce that the sea has split. Lead students across the makeshift sea to safety and celebration. Be creative and dramatic. You might give them matzah to carry or spray them with water as they approach the makeshift sea.

My D'var Torah—Trusting in God

Ask students whether they pray to God during difficult times. Tell students that throughout Jewish history, God is often referred to as "The Rock of Israel" *(Tzur Yisrael)* because God is always there to lean on and act as a source of strength for the Jewish people, even if we cannot see God.

In that way, God is like all of the people in our lives who help us to accomplish a new goal—they help us and teach us but are not physically with us when we put their lessons into practice. Have students turn to the back page of the folder. Ask students who helped them to learn to ride a bike or to swim. *(Parents, grandparents, siblings, etc.)* Then ask them, is that person with you every time you ride your bike or swim? (No) Tell students that even though these people may not physically be with them, their lessons are. So too is it with God and God's lessons.

I Think I Can

Discuss with the class how the children in the small pictures might be feeling about trying something new. Ask students to think about something new they have tried.

Bring the Value to Life: God, Nature, and Trust

Take students on a field trip outside. Point out the colorful flowers, the sweet-smelling grass, the tall trees, and the cool wind.

Ask the students, who created these plants in nature? Who causes the wind to blow? The answer is God. Even though we cannot see God directly, we can see God's creations every day. We can trust that God and God's creations are present in our lives. Ask, what are some of God's other creations that we experience every day and how else do we know that God is all around us?

I Think I Can!

It can be hard to try something new, like riding a bike the first time or learning to swim. Draw yourself trying something new.

Ask at Home

Do you remember your first day of school? What made you nervous? What made you feel better?

4

Ask at Home

Ask students about the girl in the photograph. How do they think she feels? How might the father or grandfather in the picture help the girl feel better? *(On our first day of school, we might be nervous of meeting so many new people and of making friends. Our parents' trust in us and their love can make us feel better and get through tough times.)*

The Israelites and God's Laws

Teach Me TORAH 11

Exodus 19–24

At Mount Sinai God said to Moses, "Tell the people: If you will hear My voice and obey My laws, you will be My treasured people."

And the people said, "All that God has spoken, we will do." Then they washed their clothes, made themselves ready, and waited at the foot of the mountain.

Teach Me TORAH 11

WORDS TO KNOW

Commandment—one of God's rules

Obey—to follow (a law or commandment)

Serve God—to follow God's laws and treat God's creations as we would wish to be treated

Overview

Tradition teaches that God gave the Israelites the Torah at Mount Sinai. The laws of the Torah teach us how to behave toward other people and toward God. Jewish law, which we follow today, is derived from the Torah and the teachings of Moses.

Core Concept

The Torah instructs us to serve God and obey God's laws. Today, Jewish people can serve God in many ways, including those described in the Torah and those that are part of the oral tradition.

Objectives

Students will be able to:

- Describe the atmosphere at Mount Sinai when the Torah was given
- Name at least three of the Ten Commandments
- Identify at least one way they can serve God this week
- Explain how serving God teaches us to treat others with respect

Getting Started

If you do not already have one, create a Class Contract—a list of class rules decided on by students (with teacher input) for students to sign. If you already have a list of class rules, review these rules and ask students to recommit themselves to following them.

Tell students that the Jewish people also have a list of famous rules: the Ten Commandments. These are the first ten laws that God gave to the Jewish people, and they teach them how to behave toward one another and how to follow God's rules. Ask students, why do the Jewish people need rules? How do rules help us live in peace?

Using the Illustration

After reading through the story, have students turn back to the first page. Where are the people standing? *(At Mount Sinai)* What do they think is happening at the top of the mountain? *(God is giving the laws.)* How do the people look? *(Scared, in awe, excited)*

Teaching the Story

Q. Where does the story of the Ten Commandments take place? *(Mount Sinai)*

Q. How do the Israelites prepare themselves? *(They wash their clothes and wait at the foot of Mount Sinai.)*

Q. How many commandments does God give to Moses? *(10)*

Q. What is the first commandment? *("I am the One God. You shall have no others.")*

Q. What is the fifth commandment? *("Honor your father and your mother.")*

Q. How do the Israelites promise to serve God? *(They say, "All that God has spoken, we will do.")*

Teach Me MORE Torah

As we learn in Exodus 32, while Moses was on Mount Sinai receiving the Torah, the Israelites became restless and afraid. They begged Moses' brother Aaron to give them a leader they could see. Aaron told them to collect their gold jewelry, which he then melted and used to mold a golden calf. When Moses descended Mount Sinai with the Ten Commandments, he saw the Israelites worshipping an idol. Moses was so angry he smashed the stone tablets with the Commandments inscribed on them. He then melted the idol, and ground the melted lump of gold into powder which he mixed with the Israelites' drinking water (Exodus 32:19-20). Moses cried out to God for help and to forgive the Israelites. Moses went up Mt. Sinai a second time and God gave him a second set of stone tablets.

On the third morning, the mountain was covered in clouds. Lightning flashed and thunder crashed and a blast from the shofar made the people tremble. And God came down in fire and smoke, and spoke to the Children of Israel the words of the Ten Commandments:

1. I am the One God. You shall have no others.
2. Do not make idols to pray to in My place.
3. Do not speak falsely in My name.
4. Remember Shabbat, and keep it holy.
5. Honor your father and your mother.
6. Do not murder.
7. Do not be false to your wife or husband.
8. Do not steal.
9. Do not lie about your neighbor.
10. Do not wish for your neighbor's belongings.

And the people promised to be faithful and to serve God. "All that God has spoken, we will do," they said.

God called to Moses. "Come. I have written all the laws on tablets of stone so that you can teach the people." And Moses went up the mountain to receive the tablets with God's laws.

2

Using the Illustration

Ask students to describe what is happening. What is Moses holding up? *(The stone tablets—the Ten Commandments)* How does Moses look? *(Sad, almost angry—to see why, read "Teach Me MORE Torah")*

Message at Sinai

Find and circle the words in the word bank below.

MOSES SINAI ISRAEL OBEY GOD

O	B	E	Y	I	A
M	T	G	H	E	O
N	M	O	S	E	S
O	G	D	N	E	O
D	S	I	N	A	I
I	S	R	A	E	L

Copy the red letters onto the lines below to find God's special message to the Children of Israel.

I AM THE ONE GOD.

Serving God

What does it mean to serve God?

The Torah tells us that the Israelites promised to serve God by remembering God's laws, and following them. "All that God has spoken, we will do," they said.

What will you do this week to serve God?

3

Message at Sinai

Have students complete the word search and copy the red letters which read "I am the One God." Ask students to describe the giving of the Torah in two sentences or fewer using all of the words that they found in the word search.

Bring the Story to Life: Your Own Ten Commandments

Select a few of the commandments and read them aloud to the students. Ask students to describe a situation where they might be tempted not to follow the commandment. Then, have the class write ten additional commandments they would like to include in their own lives. Their answers might include: *Be nice to your friends; share your toys;* or, *help your younger brother or sister.* Write these on poster board that is pre-cut into tablet shapes, and hang on the wall.

My D'var Torah: Serving God

Let students brainstorm as a class about how they can serve God this week. They might celebrate Shabbat or help a parent clean up after dinner. They might share a toy with a friend or decide to tell the truth even when it is difficult. Explain to students that serving God is not just performing certain actions but is also choosing *not* to perform certain actions, like stealing.

We Will Remember

Have students describe how the children depicted are serving or not serving God. How might the girl who appears to be not serving God change her ways? Begin a discussion about the power of choice. The Israelites *chose* to accept God's laws, and so can we.

Bring the Value to Life—Serving God...at Snack Time

Hand out 11 x17 inch sheets of paper to your students. Instruct them to write or draw ways they can serve God during mealtimes, such as saying a prayer before eating, saying thank you to God after eating, or sharing snacks with a friend. Set the table using these papers as placemats. At snack time, talk with students how they can serve God every day and every time they sit down to eat!

We Will Remember

Circle the pictures that show people remembering to serve God. Draw a line under the person who has forgotten to serve God.

Ask at Home

What is a good way to honor a parent?

4

Ask at Home

Begin with the photograph. What is this girl doing? How does this show honor for her parents? Ask students: what kinds of things can you do to show how you honor your parents? Some answers might be: *Help clear the dishes after dinner, give a parent a hug when he or she looks sad, or stop fighting with a sister or brother when a parent asks.*

Ruth 1–4

After her husband and her sons died in Moab, Naomi decided to return home to the Land of Israel.

"Go back to your families," Naomi said to her sons' wives. One agreed, but the other refused to leave Naomi. Her name was Ruth.

"Where you go, I will go," Ruth said to Naomi. "Your people will be my people. Your God will be my God." And she followed Naomi back to the Land of Israel.

Overview
The story of Ruth tells of a strong and caring woman who chooses to live a Jewish life in the Land of Israel. We also learn of the charity of Boaz, who provides Ruth's family with food.

Core Concept
Jewish law teaches us to honor the convert in our community and to provide food for those are in need.

Objectives
Students will be able to:

- Describe how and why Ruth joined the Jewish people
- Trace Ruth's relation to King David
- Recount how our ancestors in Israel made sure their neighbors had food to eat
- Name at least two ways that we, today, can help provide food to those in need

Teach Me TORAH 12

WORDS TO KNOW
Glean—to pick up and collect fallen grain

Convert—to choose to embrace a different religion

Getting Started
Ask students to name as many reasons as they can why they like being Jewish and list their answers on the board *(for example, eating ḥallah, lighting Shabbat candles, and celebrating Ḥanukkah)*. Prompt them to think about what Jewish values they like *(for example, giving tzedakah and welcoming guests)*. Tell students that being Jewish is not always a gift of birth. Some people choose to become Jewish as adults. The Torah teaches us to respect these people who convert to Judaism and to include them in all parts of the Jewish community. One such person is the biblical heroine, Ruth, whom they will learn about in today's lesson.

Using the Illustration
After reading through the story, have students turn back to the first page. Who are the two women? *(The older woman is Naomi; the younger woman is Ruth.)* Where are they heading? *(Land of Israel)* What season is it? *(Season of the barley harvest)*

The two women had very little food. But it was the harvest season. "I will go into the fields," said Ruth. "I will walk behind the workers and pick up grain they leave behind."

A farmer named Boaz owned the field Ruth chose. Boaz knew that Ruth and Naomi were alone and hungry. "Return only to my field," Boaz said to Ruth. Then he told his workers to leave extra grain behind for her to find. And Ruth shared all this with Naomi.

Boaz saw that Ruth was kind. He saw that she was loyal to Naomi.

"You are a fine woman," Boaz said to Ruth. "I will marry Ruth," he said to Naomi.

God blessed Ruth and Boaz. They had a son named Obed. And Obed's son was Jesse. And Jesse's son was David. And David grew up to become King of Israel. This was the blessing God gave to Ruth for being loyal to Naomi and to God, and choosing the faith of the Jews.

2

Teaching the Story

Q. **After her sons die, what does Naomi wish to do?** *(Return to the Land of Israel)*

Q. **Who accompanies Naomi to the Land of Israel?** *(Ruth, her daughter-in-law)*

Q. **What does Ruth say to show her commitment to Naomi and the Jewish people? ("Where you go, I will go. Your people will be my people. Your God will be my God.")**

Q. **In the Land of Israel, are the women wealthy? How do we know?** *(No. They do not have enough to eat.)*

Q. **Who provides food for Ruth and Naomi, and how?** *(Boaz. He tells his workers to leave extra grain behind for Ruth to gather and share with Naomi.)*

Q. **How is Ruth related to King David?** *(Ruth is King David's great-grandmother.)*

Teach Me MORE Torah

Why do we read the book of Ruth on Shavuot, a holiday that celebrates the giving of the Torah and the Ten Commandments?

The Torah teaches that when the Ten Commandments were given, the Israelites announced that they would follow God's laws and accept God's rules. The rabbis interpret this decision as a moment of conversion, meaning that the Israelites willfully and vocally acknowledge their commitment to God.

Similarly, when Ruth accompanies Naomi to the Land of Israel, she announces that she will accept God as the only God, and by extension God's rules. This is her moment of conversion.

On Shavuot, we celebrate all who have chosen to serve God and live according to God's rules, whether or not they were born Jewish.

Help Ruth Find Food

Connect the dots to help Ruth gather enough food for herself and Naomi.

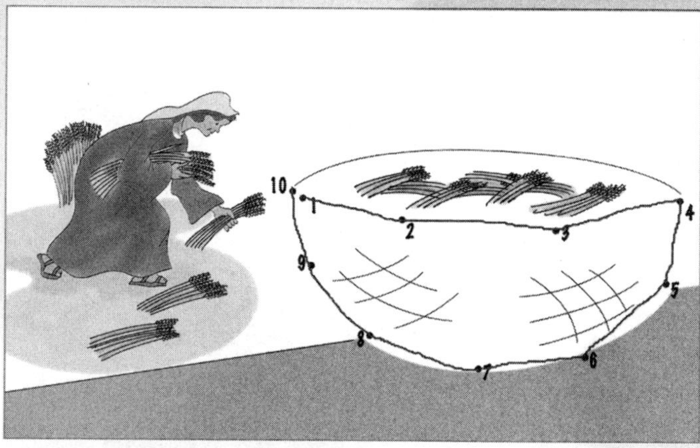

Feeding the Hungry

Why did Boaz leave grain in his fields?

It was the custom in ancient Israel for farmers to let poor people pick up fallen grain from the fields at harvest time. Picking up the fallen stalks was called gleaning. By leaving extra grain behind, Boaz helped Ruth gather enough food for herself and Naomi.

Today hungry people in our country cannot find food in a field. How can we help them?

3

Using the Illustration

Ask students to describe what is happening. What is Ruth doing? *(She is gleaning the extra grain.)* Who left this grain for Ruth? *(Boaz told his workers to leave the grain.)*

Help Ruth Find Food

Have students connect the dots to display a basket of barely sheaves. Ask students, how might Ruth have felt receiving help from Boaz? How might Boaz have helped Ruth feel comfortable gleaning from his fields?

Bring the Story to Life: Giving Away Barley ... and Candy

Bring this harvest narrative to life by bringing in raw barley to show the students (barley is available at most supermarkets). Distribute a little barley to each student. Remind students that in ancient times farmers would give a portion of their grain to the poor so that everyone would have food to eat. Instruct them to set aside a portion of their barley.

Next, distribute candy. Instruct students once again to set aside a portion of their candy to give to underprivileged children. Ask students if setting aside the candy was as easy as setting aside the barley. Remind them that, in ancient times, food was not always plentiful and barley was just as desirable as candy and was not something given away without thought.

My D'var Torah: Feeding the Hungry

Let students brainstorm ideas for how they can help feed the hungry, such as *organizing a food drive, asking parents to clean out a pantry and donate unopened food, or giving tzedakah to an organization, such as Mazon, that is committed to fighting world hunger.*

The Helping Path

Ask students how providing a warm coat for someone who is cold or a teddy bear to a crying baby is like giving food to the hungry. You might wish to introduce the idea of giving everyone the tools they need in order to live happy and healthy lives.

Bring the Value to Life: BIG Tzedakah Box

Explain to students that, like tzedakah itself, tzedakah boxes come in all shapes and sizes. Instruct students to decorate a large cardboard box. Designate it as the "BIG Tzedakah Box." Fill the box not with coins but with cans of food.

Send a note home to parents and ask students to donate food every Friday before Shabbat. Remind them to bring both food staples *and* tasty treats; that is, to donate the same type of food that they themselves would wish to eat.

Ask at Home

Be sure to approach this question sensitively as there may be children of people who converted in your class. It is a good idea to have a story of your own about someone who is "like Ruth" in case no one in the class is able to say "yes." Ask students how they can help welcome such newcomers to the community. You may wish to help students begin this conversation with their parents with the question, "How can we welcome new people into our community?"

Teach Me
TORAH
13

I Samuel 17

Israel was at war. The enemy had a secret weapon. It was a giant named Goliath.

"Who will fight against me?" roared Goliath. No one wanted to fight a giant. Everyone was afraid. But a boy named David was not afraid.

David's brothers were soldiers. David was a shepherd. He kept wild animals away from his father's sheep. Sometimes he killed them with his slingshot.

Overview

David is brave and trusts in God. Even though he is just a young shepherd, he defeats the giant Goliath and leads the Israelites to a great victory.

Core Concept

Being brave means trusting in ourselves, in others, and in God.

Objectives

Students will be able to:

- Name the young shepherd who defeated the giant Goliath
- Describe the means by which David defeated Goliath *(a slingshot and single stone)*
- Identify ways they themselves can act bravely
- Complete the sentence: "I am brave when I …"

WORDS TO KNOW

Shepherd—someone who looks after sheep

Getting Started

Tell students that you are going to be doing a little acting before class and that they are going to be stretching their facial muscles. Ask them first to make a face that shows that they are happy. Then, make a face that shows that they're sad. Finally, make a face to show that they are brave. Tell them that everyone can be brave—no matter what they look like, how big they are, or how old they are. For example, Jewish tradition teaches us about David, a young, small shepherd who defeated a giant named Goliath.

Using the Illustration 1

After reading through the story, have students turn back to the first page. Can they find elements from the story? Which character is David? *(The small, young boy)* Which character is Goliath? *(The large warrior)* Does David look scared? *(No. He looks confident and brave.)* How would they have felt standing opposite Goliath?

Teaching the Story

Q. **What the secret weapon of Israel's enemy?** *(Goliath, the giant)*

Q. **Who agreed to fight Goliath?** *(David)*

Q. **David's brothers were soldiers, but David was not. What did David do?** *(He was a shepherd.)*

Q. **Why is David not afraid to fight Goliath? What makes him brave?** *(David trusts that God will help him, just as God helps him to protect his sheep from wild animals.)*

Q. **What weapon does David use to defeat Goliath?** *(A slingshot)* **Is it big?** *(No.)*

Q. **Who does David grow up to be?** *(The king of Israel)*

Teach Me MORE Torah

David comes from an important biblical family. He is the great-grandson of Ruth. His son Solomon also becomes king and builds the Holy Temple *(Beit HaMikdash)* in Jerusalem. Tradition also teaches us that the messiah will be a descendent of David's. David's whole family plays a big role in Jewish history and Jewish legend. David himself goes on to be the king of Israel and makes a name for himself as a warrior, musician, and poet.

One day David took food to his brothers. He saw Goliath. He heard Goliath's booming voice. He saw that the soldiers were afraid to fight the giant.

David was not afraid. "God helped me kill a lion and a bear," he said. "With God's help I know I can kill a giant." David took his shepherd's stick. He took his slingshot. He took a bag filled with smooth stones. And he set out to fight Goliath.

Goliath laughed when he saw David. "Do you think you can stop me with a stick?" he roared.

"I will stop you with God's help," said David.

David took a stone from his bag and put it in his slingshot. Carefully he aimed. Then sent the stone flying. It hit Goliath right in the middle of his forehead. The giant fell to the ground.

David had killed Goliath. The war was over. The Israelites had won. And this small, brave boy would someday become king of Israel.

2

Using the Illustration

Ask students to describe what is happening. What is David swinging? *(His slingshot)* Who is his target? *(Goliath)* What do you think is going through David's mind right now? *(Answers will vary and might include: he is scared; he is confident and brave; or, he is focused.)*

A Giant Fight

Circle three things David took with him to fight Goliath.

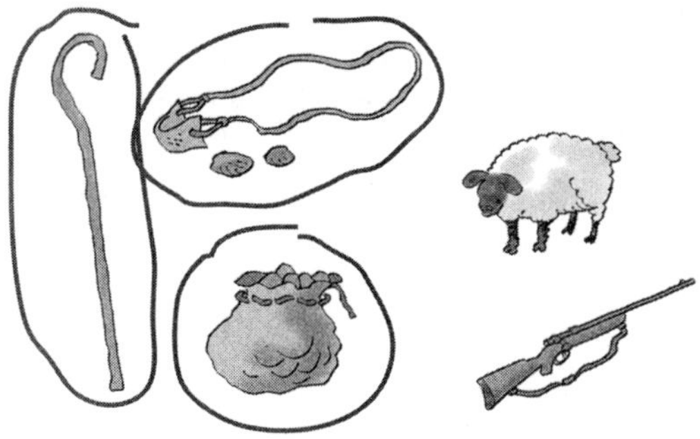

David also took something no one could see. Do you know what it was?

Being Brave

What made David brave?

Our tradition tells us that David felt God helping him protect his father's sheep from wild animals. David said he was not afraid of Goliath because he knew God would help him fight the giant too.

What helps you be brave?

3

A Giant Fight

Make sure students can identify all the objects in the activity. After students complete the circling activity, ask the whole class to answer the follow-up question concerning God's presence with David. Ask them to think of a moment when they were facing a great challenge. What physical items did they take with them? *(A pen for a test, a soccer ball to practice with before the big game)* What invisible items did they take with them? *(Their parents' love, years of practice, a memory of encouraging words)* Prompt your students to think about all the invisible sources of strength and support in their lives.

Bring the Story to Life: Cheering David On

Ask students to describe the moments leading up to David and Goliath's battle. What did the scene look like? Who was there? Remind students that David was not alone on the battlefield but was surrounded by Israelite soldiers—not to mention Goliath's supporters. Tell students to pretend that they are David's supporters watching him as he prepares to fight Goliath. Instruct them to create cheers for David to encourage him during the fight. Just as God and the Israelites supported David, so too can students motivate the young shepherd.

My D'var Torah: Being Brave

Ask students why they chose as they did. Did they choose something that makes them feel safe or lucky, such as a favorite necklace or baseball hat? Is it something invisible, such as good advice? Is what helps them similar to what helped David?

Call It Courage

Have students discuss the two vignettes pictured before completing their drawings (or taking turns describing themselves being brave.) Ask students to share their drawings or ideas with the class. How did they portray themselves? What type of situation did each draw or describe?

Bring the Value to Life: Leading Shabbat Prayers

One of the biggest fears reported by people in our country today is the fear of public speaking. Let students demonstrate being brave by preparing them to lead a prayer on Shabbat. Choose a prayer to teach the students with input from the school's rabbi or cantor. Invite parents to a special Shabbat services in which the rabbi will invite the students up to the *bimah*. Before the big day, spend time in class teaching the melody and meaning of the prayer. Consider inviting the cantor to class to teach the prayer. You might also ask the rabbi or cantor to say a few words during services about what the children are studying *(David and Goliath)* and the lessons they are learning *(to be brave for the Jewish people).*

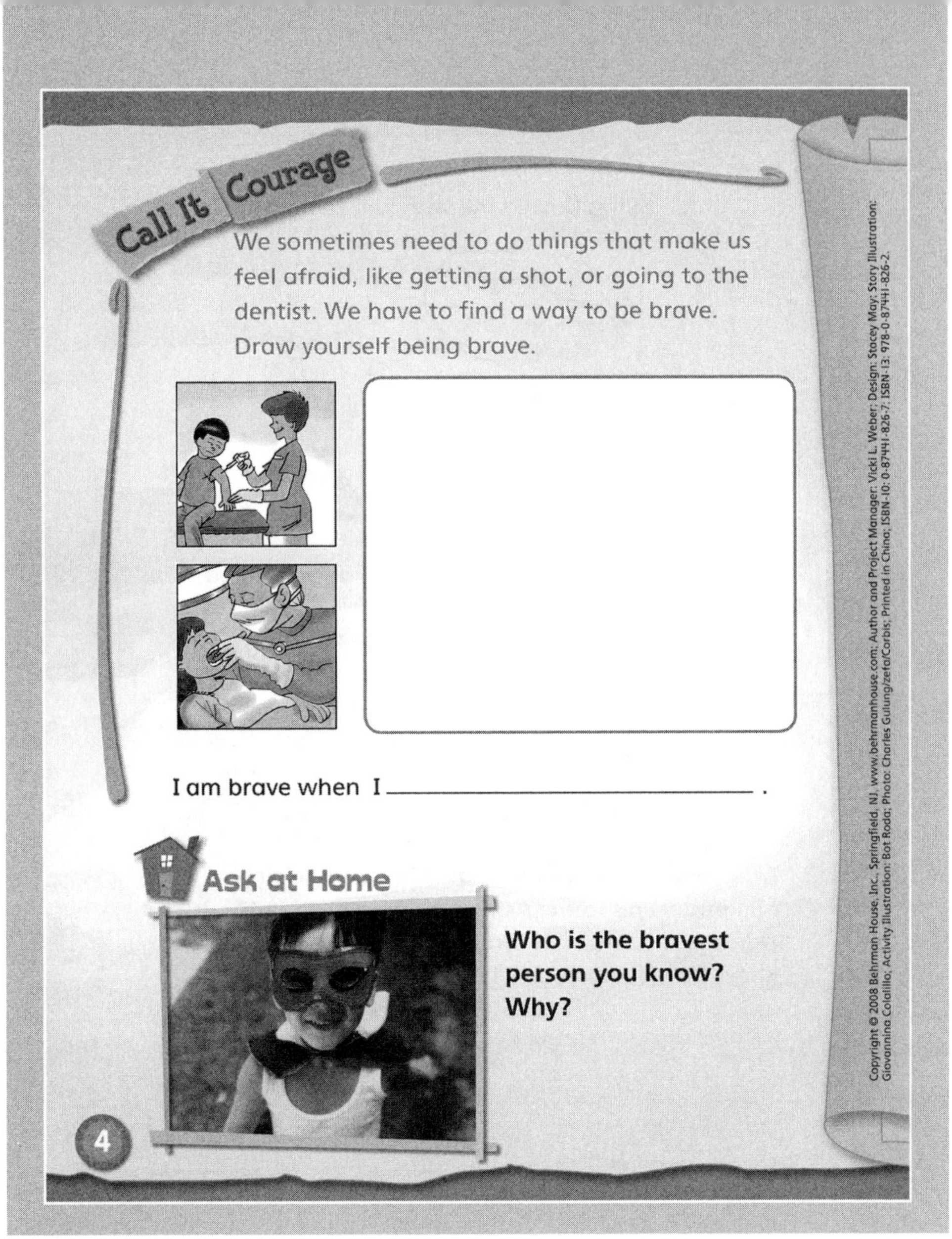
Call It Courage

We sometimes need to do things that make us feel afraid, like getting a shot, or going to the dentist. We have to find a way to be brave. Draw yourself being brave.

I am brave when I ______________.

Ask at Home

Who is the bravest person you know? Why?

4

Ask at Home

Begin by discussing the photograph of a boy dressed up as a superhero. How are superheroes brave? Ask students follow-up questions that lead to at-home discussions such as: Who is the bravest person in your family? When have you seen a parent act bravely? When have you done something brave for your family?

Teach Me TORAH 14

Solomon

I Kings 3

Solomon, Israel's third king, did not dream of riches, or long life, or death for his enemies.

King Solomon's dream was to take care of the people of Israel with wisdom.

One day, two women came before King Solomon. "We live in the same house," said the first woman. "I had a baby. Three days later, she had a baby. But her baby died. That night I saw her take my baby and put the dead one in its place. Make her give my baby back!"

Overview

King Solomon is renowned for his wisdom and sense of justice. He is often faced with complex cases and seeks creative solutions. For example, the case brought by the two women at first appears unsolvable. However, King Solomon discovers the truth using quick thinking and close observation.

Core Concept

Seeking wisdom, as demonstrated by King Solomon, involves asking questions and finding answers to difficult problems.

Objectives

Students will be able to:

- Name the wise king of Israel
- Give an example of King Solomon's wisdom
- Identify wise individuals in their own lives
- Describe at least three places to seek wisdom

Teach Me TORAH 14

WORDS TO KNOW

Wisdom—knowledge gained from experience; good judgment

Getting Started

Tell students to imagine that they are kings or queens living in ancient Israel. What would they wish to possess? *(Great palaces, jewels, etc.)* What would they need to rule their kingdom? *(Laws, an army, good advisors)* What might they pray to God to grant them? *(Courage, riches)*

Tell students that the Torah teaches that when King Solomon began to rule ancient Israel, God came to him in a dream and asked him what he desired. King Solomon did not respond that he wished for something physical or materialistic. Instead, King Solomon wished for wisdom so that he might rule fairly over his kingdom.

Using the Illustration

Have students identify the characters in the story. Who is holding the baby? *(King Solomon)* *Who is the crying woman? (The baby's mother)* How does the woman pretending to be the baby's mother look? *(Mean, smug)* Ask students how they think King Solomon must have felt while judging this case. What might the picture suggest?

Teaching the Story

Q. What did King Solomon wish to possess? *(Wisdom)*

Q. Who came before King Solomon?
(Two women, each claiming to be the mother of a baby)

Q. How did King Solomon uncover the real mother?
(He announced that he would cut the baby in half. The real mother begged King Solomon not to do so.)

Q. Why did the real mother beg King Solomon not to cut the baby in half?
(She did not want him to hurt her son.)

Teach Me MORE Torah

How did King Solomon become wise? God granted King Solomon wisdom (1 Kings 3:12).

God granted biblical heroes many gifts, such as bravery, leadership skills, and wisdom. However, King Solomon had to work to make this gift succeed. He had to actively work to grow in wisdom and knowledge.

Consider turning this lesson into a discussion about how we are partners with God. God may grant many gifts to human beings but it is up to us to use these gifts and develop them.

"No!" said the second woman. "The live baby is my son! The dead one is yours."

"Bring a sword!" ordered King Solomon. "I will cut this baby in two. Each of you will get half. That will be fair."

"I agree," said the second woman. "Then the baby will be neither hers nor mine."

But the first woman began to cry. "No! Please! No!" she begged. "Give the baby to her, then. Just please don't hurt him."

King Solomon now knew the truth. "You would rather give your son away than let him be hurt," he said to the crying woman. "I know you are his real mother." And King Solomon let the crying woman keep her baby.

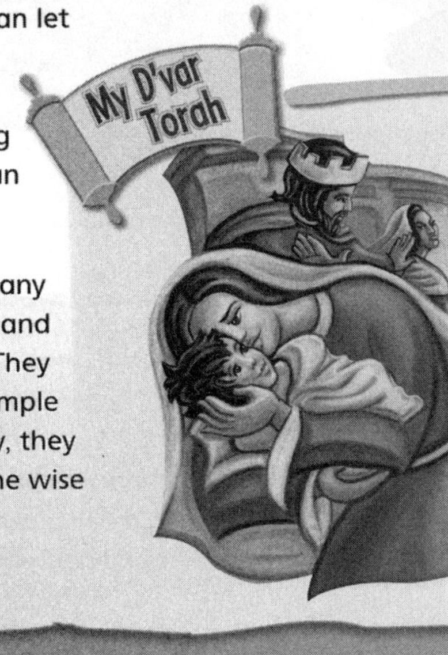

Solomon ruled in Israel for many years. His decisions were just and wise. The people loved him. They helped him build the Holy Temple in Jerusalem. And even today, they tell stories about Solomon, the wise king of Israel.

2

Using the Illustration 2

Ask students to describe what is happening. Who is holding the baby? *(the baby's real mother)* What is King Solomon doing? *(He is keeping the other woman away.)*

Whose Baby?

Help King Solomon return the baby to its real mother.

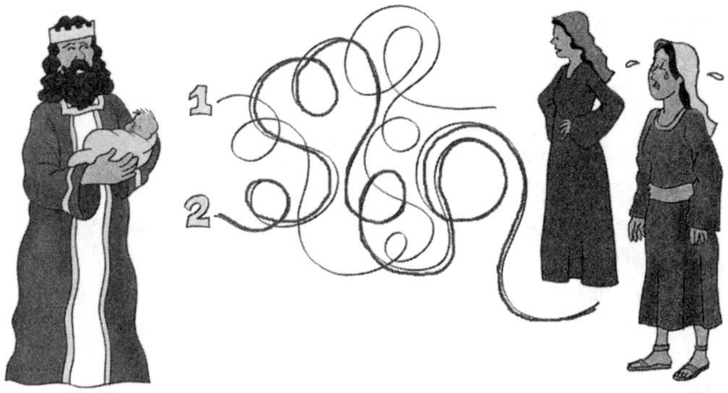

Seeking Wisdom

What made Solomon a great king?

Solomon did not ask for money. He did not want God to kill his enemies for him. Solomon wanted to be able to help his people. He wanted wisdom.

Think of someone you know who is wise. How can you tell?

3

Whose Baby?

Ask students if it is difficult to decide who the real mother is. What are some clues from the story that help? *(The story says the real mother was the crying woman).*

Ask students if they can think of any other way that King Solomon might have been able to decide who the baby's real mother was.

Bring the Story to Life: Wise Eyes ... and Ears ...

Begin a discussion about decision-making. Ask: what senses did King Solomon use to make his decision? *(Hearing—he listened to answers; Sight—he saw the real mother cry.)*

Ask students, what senses do they use to make wise decisions? For example, how do they know what to wear when they get up in the morning? Do they look outside to see if it's raining? Do they step outside to feel the temperature? Do they ask their parents for a weather update?

My D'var Torah: Seeking Wisdom

Ask students: What makes someone wise? Have you seen them make decisions? What is the process? Then ask students how they can learn from these wise individuals. For answers, turn to the back page of the folder.

Ways to Wisdom

Have students discuss what is happening in each vignette. *(Children listening to a grandmother tell stories about her life; students doing a science experiment; studying Torah; shopping for toys)* Ask: where else can we turn to learn more and become wise people?

Bring the Value to Life: Wise Rabbis

Tell students that Judaism has always valued the wisdom of its leaders—kings, rabbis, and teachers. Invite the synagogue rabbi—a wise figure—to read a story about wisdom to the children.

For ideas, check out *Three Times Chai* (Behrman House 2006). Some popular tales include those of the Wise Men of Chelm. These silly wise men have many lessons to teach about the nature of wisdom and how to think outside of the box.

Following the story, ask students to describe the meaning of wisdom and brainstorm ways that they can grow up to be wise people.

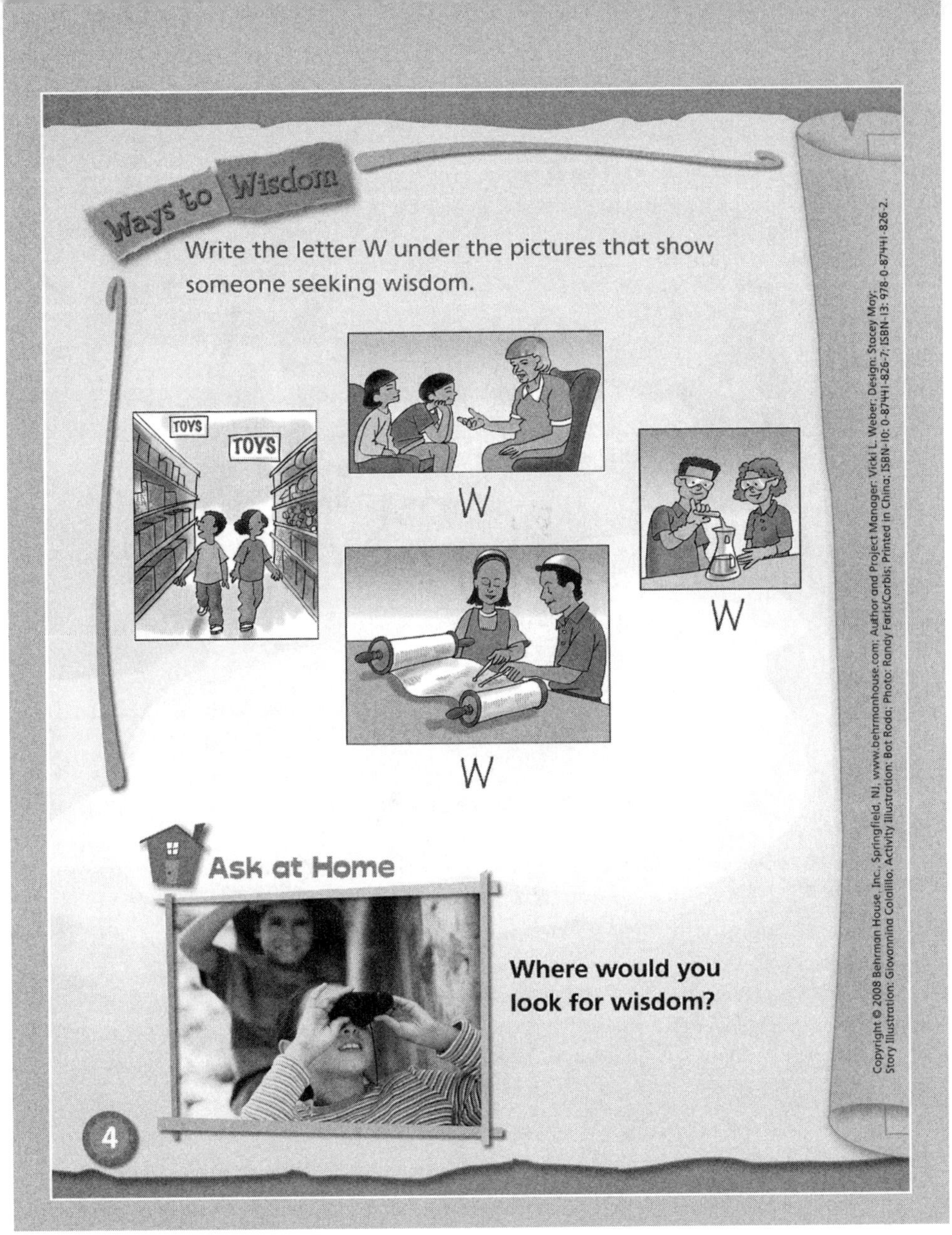

Ways to Wisdom

Write the letter W under the pictures that show someone seeking wisdom.

Ask at Home

Where would you look for wisdom?

4

Ask at Home

Ask students about the photograph. What are these children doing? Is this the right way to search for wisdom? Ask students: Who in your family is wise? What can you learn from him or her? Where in your house can you look for wisdom? *(Computer, bookshelf)* Ask them to find out where their parents look for wisdom.

Jonah 1–4

God called Jonah to be a prophet. "Go to Nineveh," God said. "Tell the people I will destroy the city for their evil ways."

But Jonah did not want to be a prophet. So he ran away. He took a boat to sail far from God.

God sent a storm to follow the boat. The wind blew and waves crashed all around it. The sailors on the boat were terrified.

Teach Me TORAH 15

WORDS TO KNOW

Prophet—a person who relays God's messages

Prediction—a statement about the future

Getting Started

Bring newspapers and news magazines to class. Read some of the headlines with the students. When they come to a headline about people who are suffering, be it from war or hunger, ask them why it is important to read the newspaper and learn about these stories.

Ask students to consider why it is important to care about others, even if we do not know them and will never meet them. Explain to students that we learn the importance of caring about others, even those who behave differently from us, in the story of Jonah.

Using the Illustration

Have students investigate the elements of the illustration. What is happening to Jonah? *(He is about to be swallowed by the big fish)* Does the sea look calm? *(No. It's stormy. The waves are high.)* Can they find the boat? Ask students to describe what happens next.

Overview

Jonah struggles as God's prophet. First, he runs away. Then, he becomes angry after God's decision to forgive the people of Nineveh. Jonah's story demonstrates that following God's laws is not always easy, but these laws teach us how to care for others.

Core Concept

When people behave poorly, we must care for them and help them to change their ways. And, when they change their ways, it's our job to forgive their past wrongdoings.

Objectives

Students will be able to:

- Identify a biblical character who struggled to obey God
- Recount Jonah's indirect route to Nineveh
- Differentiate between forgiving someone and holding a grudge
- Describe ways to persevere through unwanted tasks

Teaching the Story

Q. What did God want Jonah to tell the people of Nineveh? *(God wanted Jonah to tell them that God would destroy the city because of their evil ways.)*

Q. Did Jonah want to be God's prophet? How do we know? *(No. He tried to sail far away.)*

Q. Why did the weather turn stormy when Jonah got on the boat? *(Jonah had disobeyed God.)*

Q. What happened to Jonah when he went overboard? *(He was swallowed by a huge fish. He prayed to God after he spent three days inside the fish.)*

Q. Where did Jonah go when he got out of the big fish and why? *(Jonah went to Nineveh to give them God's warning.)*

Q. Did the people of Nineveh listen to Jonah? *(Yes. They repented.)*

Q. Was Jonah happy that God forgave the people of Nineveh? Why or why not? *(No. He was embarrassed and worried that he would look foolish because his prediction had not come true.)*

"Throw me overboard," said Jonah. "The fault is mine." So the sailors threw Jonah into the sea.

A huge fish swallowed Jonah. For three days Jonah was trapped inside. Jonah prayed to God, and the fish spit him out onto dry land.

"Now go to Nineveh!" God said to Jonah. This time, Jonah went.

"In forty days God will destroy this city!" Jonah shouted as he walked through the streets of Nineveh. The people heard Jonah and believed his words. They turned from their evil ways, and asked God for mercy.

And so God did not destroy Nineveh after all.

Jonah's prediction had not come true. This made him angry. "I would rather die than live," he said.

"Are you angry because I did not punish the people of Nineveh?" God asked. "Should I not care about people who are trying to learn right from wrong?"

2

Teach Me MORE Torah 1

What swallowed Jonah? We often hear this story referred to as "Jonah and the Whale." Here, we refer to the sea creature as a "huge fish." Why?

The original Hebrew phrase, *dag gadol,* means "big fish." The term "whale" became popular only after a Latin translation of the text described the animal as a whale. This confusion of terms shows how helpful it can be to go back to the Hebrew original for clarification.

Did the fish really swallow Jonah? This story, like many in the Bible, contains unlikely details and helps remind us that our tradition is an oral one. Stories handed down orally can grow or change in the telling and retelling.

Our tradition takes this and its other stories seriously not because of any specific details, but because of what they teach about human nature, about how we should live, and about our relationship with God.

Using the Illustration 2

Ask students to describe what is happening. How does Jonah look? *(Angry)* Why does he seem angry? *(He is angry because God forgave the people of Nineveh)* Ask students why they think Jonah might have gotten when his prediction did not come true. *(He was embarrassed; he felt foolish because people thought he lied.)* Ask students: how would you have felt if you were Jonah?

Rescue at Sea Word Search

Find and circle the words shown in the word bank. Copy the **red** letters onto the spaces below to see who was trying to hide.

Word Bank

BOAT	STORM		FISH
SAIL	WIND	RUN	SEA

F	I	S	H	J
W	O	T	M	P
I	B	O	A	T
N	S	R	U	N
D	E	M	A	L
S	A	I	L	H

J O N A H

Caring about Others

Jonah's words saved the city of Nineveh. Why was he angry that God did not destroy it?

Jonah told the people of Nineveh they would be destroyed for their evil ways. His words helped them change their ways. But Jonah was angry that his prediction did not come true. He cared more about being right than about saving the people of Nineveh.

When someone makes a mistake, what is more important, punishment or forgiveness? Why?

3

Teach Me MORE Torah 2

Look at the illustration on pages 2 and 3. Notice that Jonah is standing under a tree. That is the *kikayon,* often translated as the *ricinus* or castor oil plant. Other traditions hold that the *kikayon* refers to a gourd plant.

The Bible teaches that after Jonah got upset with God for forgiving the people of Nineveh, he made himself a shelter under the *kikayon.* God caused the plant to grow and provide shade, which made Jonah happy. Then, God caused the plant to die and the sun beat down on Jonah, who begged for death. God admonishes Jonah. After all, Jonah cared deeply for the plant even though he did not help the *kikayon* grow and merely complained when it died. If Jonah could care so much for the *kikayon,* should not God then care for the people of Nineveh?

Rescue at Sea Word Search

You can make this a class activity by copying the word search grid onto the board or onto a large piece of poster paper. Be sure to copy the red letters in a different color. Ask students if the colored letters were hard to find. Then ask students if Jonah would have been hard to find. Do they think God always knew where he was? Do they think that Jonah really wanted to hide? Encourage students to understand the story on their own terms.

Bring the Story to Life: Inside the Whale

Draw a large outline of a giant fish on a piece of butcher paper. Invite the students to stand inside the outline and pretend that they are in the stomach of a giant fish. Ask them: What does it look like? What does it smell like? Are they scared? Why might Jonah have been scared? What should they do to get out of the fish? What prayers might they say? You may wish to tell students that, in their class, the way to get out of the fish is to show that they care for their fellow students. Let each student thank his or her neighbor for something he or she did that week.

My D'var Torah: Caring about Others

Ask students: How do you show you care about someone? Do you help with a job? Do you give the person a hug? Then ask students how it feels to forgive someone and how it feels to hold a grudge. Which is a Jewish value—accepting an apology or holding a grudge? What does the story of Jonah teach us to do?

Show You Care

After discussing the two vignettes, ask students how they help take care of each other, and specifically how they help ensure each other's safety. You may wish to turn this lesson into a discussion on staying safe and looking out for everyone in your community.

Bring the Value to Life: Get Well Mini-Posters

Tell students that caring for others can take many forms. You can care for your family, people who are hungry, and people who are sick. Create 8 ½ x 11 inch get well mini-posters. Before class, photocopy a sheet of paper which reads "Get well soon!" or *"Refu'ah shleimah"* (a full recovery). Teach students this Hebrew phrase.

After the students decorate the poster, send it to sick or injured members of the community. You may wish to ask one of the poster recipients to send you a picture of that person holding the poster. This will allow students to see the results of their efforts.

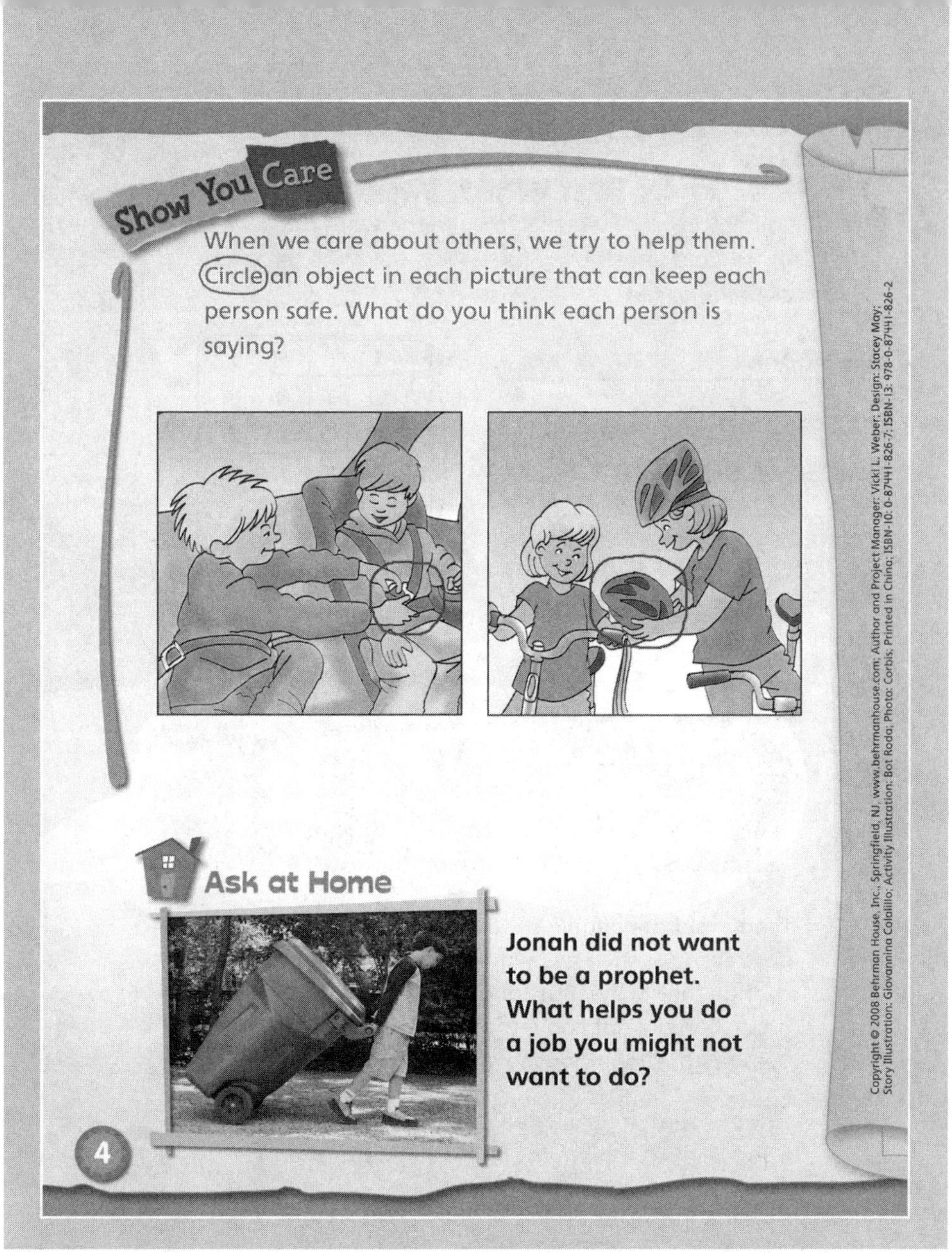
Show You Care

When we care about others, we try to help them. Circle an object in each picture that can keep each person safe. What do you think each person is saying?

Ask at Home

Jonah did not want to be a prophet. What helps you do a job you might not want to do?

4

Story Illustration: Giovannina Colalillo; Activity Illustration: Bot Roda; Photo: Corbis; Printed in China; ISBN-10: 0-87441-826-7; ISBN-13: 978-0-87441-826-2

Ask at Home

You may wish to tie this question to the lesson on "Caring about Others" by talking about the need to care for yourself. We all face challenges and must work to overcome those challenges.

Ask students follow-up questions that lead to at-home discussions such as: What jobs do you do at home that you do not want to do? How do you feel once you've finished the job? How do you feel when someone says thank you?

Esther I–7

Esther had a secret.

The king had chosen Esther to be his queen. He knew he loved her. He knew that Esther and her cousin Mordechai had stopped an evil plot to kill him. But the king did not know Esther's secret. He did not know that she was a Jew.

Haman was the king's advisor. The people of the city had to bow before him. But Mordechai would bow only before God. This filled the proud Haman with rage.

Overview

Esther is the queen. She is also Jewish. When the Jewish people of her kingdom are threatened, Esther risks her own life and comes to their aid.

Core Concept

Kol Yisrael areivim zeh bazeh: All Jewish people are responsible for one another, in good times and bad.

Objectives

Students will be able to:

- Name a Jewish heroine who saved the Jewish people
- Distinguish between Mordechai and Haman
- Identify at least three ways to show loyalty to the Jewish people today
- Begin to discuss what living as a Jew in a non-Jewish society means

Teach Me TORAH 16

WORDS TO KNOW

Loyalty—feeling of duty and attachment

King Ahasuerus—the king (unnamed in the text)

Shushan—the city in the Persian empire where the king and Esther lived (unnamed in the text)

Getting Started

Ask students what blessings Jewish people in their community say on Shabbat. Then, ask students what blessings Jewish people say in Israel on Shabbat. What about Jewish people in England? In Russia? In Morocco?

Ask students if they are surprised to learn that Jewish people around the world all say the same blessings. They are part of one large community—the Jewish community. It is up to us to maintain and protect that community and remain loyal to the Jewish people.

Using the Illustration

Have students identify all the characters pictured: *(from left to right: Mordechai, Queen Esther, King Ahasuerus, Haman)* Ask: What do you think Mordechai is feeling? *(Nervous)* What is Haman doing? *(Giving evil advice to the king)*

Explain to students that Mordechai was very close to Esther, just as Haman was close to the king.

Teaching the Story

Q. Who was Esther?
(She was the queen.)

Q. What was her secret?
(She hid her Jewish identity.)

Q. Who was Mordechai? How did he save the King?
(Mordechai was Esther's cousin. He stopped an evil plot to kill the King.)

Q. Why did Haman get angry at the Jewish people?
(Haman was angry that Mordechai, a Jew, refused to bow down to him.)

Q. Who was Haman? What was he plotting? *(Haman was the king's advisor. He wanted to kill the Jewish people.)*

Q. How was Esther brave?
(She risked her life by going before the king, telling the king she was a Jew, and asking him to save the Jewish people.)

Q. How did Esther save the day? She made a feast for the king.
(She asked the king to save her life and the lives of all Jewish people.)

"The Jews refuse to obey your laws," Haman said to the king. "If it please Your Majesty, I will choose a day to execute them all."

The Jews of the city were terrified. "You must speak to the king!" Mordechai begged Esther. "Even your own life will be in danger."

Esther made feasts to honor the king. This made him very happy. "Whatever you wish will be yours," he said.

"I wish for my life," said Esther. "I wish for Mordechai's life, and the lives of my people. There is a man who plans to destroy us all."

"Who dares?" said the King. "You are my queen. Mordechai saved my life!"

"We are also Jews," said Esther, "And Haman plans to kill us all."

"Then let Haman be the one to die!" ordered the king.

And so each year Jews tell the story of how Queen Esther revealed her secret and saved the Jewish people.

2

Teach Me MORE Torah

We read the story of Queen Esther every year at the holiday of Purim. The word Purim means "lots." This refers to the manner in which Haman chose the date on which he planned to kill the Jewish people. Esther saved the Jewish people and we celebrate her efforts and the survival of the Jewish people on Purim.

Esther lived among non-Jewish people but she maintained her Jewish identity. One way many of us maintain that identity is by having Hebrew names. These are the names that are used when we are called up to the Torah. Ask students if they know what their Hebrew name is. Feel free to share your own Hebrew name.

Tell students that Queen Esther had a second name. It was also Hebrew. This name was *Hadassah,* which means "myrtle," a type of plant. Her other name, "Esther," appears to have Persian roots meaning "star."

Fit for a King

Esther wants to make a fabulous feast for the king so he will grant her wish. Help her by drawing some favorite foods to complete her banquet.

How do YOU feel when someone makes your favorite food for you?

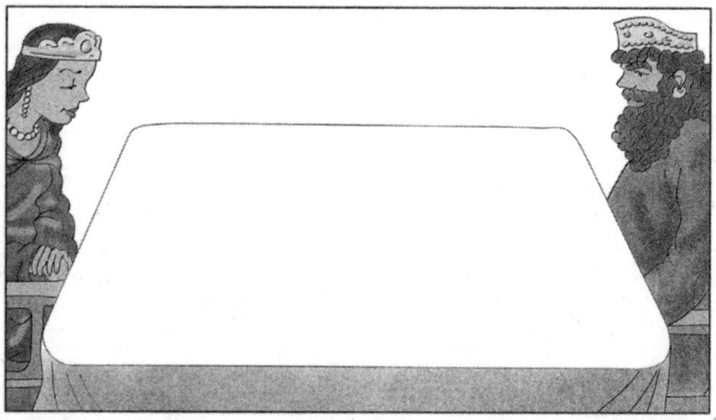

Loyalty to the Jewish People

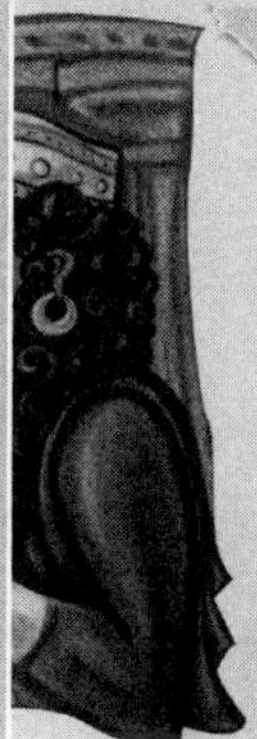

How did Esther show her loyalty to the Jewish people?

Esther did not stand by and let Haman hurt the Jews. Esther made the king feel happy, and then told him her secret. She told the king she was a Jew, too. She made the king care about her people. She saved them from the evil Haman.

How can you show loyalty to the Jewish people?

3

Using the Illustration 2

Ask students to describe what is happening. What are the king and queen doing? *(Eating at a feast)* Who invited the king to the feast? *(Esther)*

Why do you think Esther asked the king for help at a feast? *(She showed she cared for the king and made him feel comfortable with good food.)* Ask students if they think that Esther chose a good place to ask the king for help.

Fit for a King

Ask students if the activity was hard to complete. What foods did they draw? Encourage them to add traditional Jewish food to the feast table, such as *ḥallah* or *hamantashen.* Ask students what they might add if they knew that a king was coming to eat at their table.

Bring the Story to Life: Queen Esther's Royal Feast

Invite students to Queen Esther's royal feast. Provide students with arts and crafts materials to make crowns that they will wear during the meal.

At the feast, you may wish to serve *hamantashen,* the traditional Purim cookie associated with the story of Queen Esther. The triangular cookie reminds us of Haman's tri-cornered hat. At the feast, ask students what makes them, like Queen Esther, proud to be Jewish.

My D'var Torah: Loyalty to the Jewish People

Ask students what they do to show loyalty to the Jewish people every week? *(They go to religious school.)* Is it always easy to show loyalty? *(No, but it's important.)*

Color Me Loyal

Ask students which of these activities they do. Which would they like to do? Also, pose the question about the Queen Esther's holiday—Purim. Ask students how they celebrate Purim. You may wish to have a mini-Purim lesson to compliment this folder. See *Let's Discover the Holidays Teacher's Edition* (Behrman House, 1997) for suggestions.

Bring the Value to Life—Israel in Our Hearts

Connect students to the land and people of Israel. Tell students that Jewish people live all over the world. Many live in the Jewish state, Israel. Organize an Israel-themed party for your class. Serve Israeli food (falafel and Israeli chocolates), sing Hebrew songs, and decorate the room with pictures of Israeli sites.

You may wish to tell students that their "ticket" to the Israeli party is to bring something special they would like to include in a package to Israeli soldiers—some candy to munch on, a baseball hat to wear, or a great CD. Search "sending care packages to Israeli soldiers" online for instructions on how to send these gifts overseas.

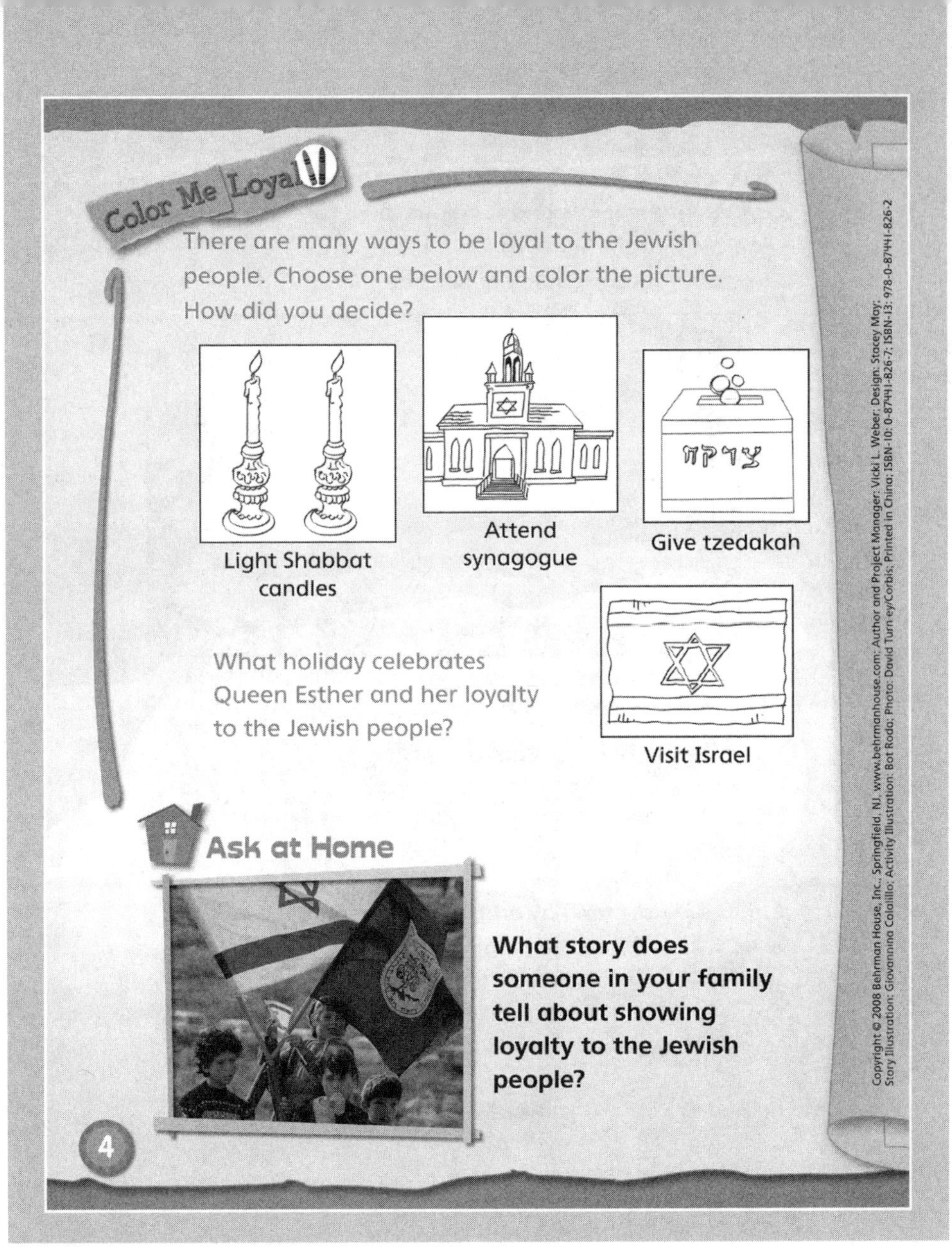

Ask at Home

You may wish to point students' attention to the photograph. Can they find the Israeli flag? Begin this discussion in class by sharing your own story about showing loyalty to Israel. Perhaps you have a relative who served in the army or who made *aliyah*—moved to Israel—either before or after the State was founded. Tell students to ask their families about this and to bring the stories they hear to share in the next class.